Women of Brave Mettle

Caitlin Press Inc.
8100 Alderwood Road,
Halfmoon Bay, BC V0N 1Y1
www.caitlin-press.com

Edited by Rebecca Hendry.
Typeset by Vici Johnstone.
Cover design by Vici Johnstone.
Printed in Canada.

Caitlin Press Inc. acknowledges financial support from the Government of Canada through the Canada Book Fund and the Canada Council for the Arts, and from the Province of British Columbia through the British Columbia Arts Council and the Book Publisher's Tax Credit.

Canada Council for the Arts   **Conseil des Arts du Canada**   BRITISH COLUMBIA ARTS COUNCIL
We acknowledge the support of the Province of British Columbia through the British Columbia Arts Council

Library and Archives Canada Cataloguing in Publication

French, Diana
        Women of brave mettle : more stories from the
Cariboo Chilcotin / Diana French.

(Extraordinary women ; 2)
ISBN 978-1-894759-86-1

        1. Women—British Columbia—Cariboo Region—Biography.
2. Women—British Columbia—Chilcotin River Region—Biography.
3. Cariboo Region (B.C.)—Biography. 4. Chilcotin River Region
(B.C.)—Biography. I. Title. II. Series: Extraordinary women
(Halfmoon Bay, B.C.) ; 2

FC3845.C3Z48 2012   971.1'75030922   C2012-903337-5

EXTRAORDINARY WOMEN VOL. 2

Women of Brave Mettle

More Stories from the Cariboo Chilcotin

Diana French

CAITLIN PRESS

Contents

Foreword

*I*t is quite fitting that Diana French took up the torch to write *Women of Brave Mettle*, the second volume of Caitlin Press's *Extraordinary Women of the Cariboo Chilcotin* series. She's been there, done that.

Diana has lived with water buckets and wood stoves, sat on various boards of directors and spent years working at the *Williams Lake Tribune*. Her personal involvement with a wide variety of community groups and individuals in more than six decades in the region has put her in contact with women from all walks of life.

The exploits of men in the Cariboo Chilcotin have been well documented. The accomplishments of women, not so much. That's what spurred the Women's Contact Society of Williams Lake to initiate a project in 2004 to collect women's stories. Women were invited to write about their own lives or to allow others to write about them. Then for three or four years this collection of two dozen stories sat in a box.

In late 2008 I got seconded into editing this material for publication. In spring of 2009, Caitlin Press publisher Vici Johnstone got wind of our project and expressed an interest in publishing it. She encouraged us to expand the number of stories, and the resulting anthology included the work of twenty-three writers and the stories of thirty-eight women. In the fall of 2009 Caitlin released *Gumption & Grit: Women of the Cariboo Chilcotin, Extraordinary Women Volume One* and it was a bestseller in the region.

It was obvious from the onset that *Gumption & Grit* only scratched the surface. There were many more women whose stories deserved to be told.

As well as her newspaper background, Diana French is the author of two books, *The Road Runs West* (Harbour Publishing, 1994) and *Ranchland* with Rick Blacklaws (Harbour Publishing, 2001). She wrote the foreword to Gumption & Grit, and is one of the women featured in the anthology, so it was a natural fit for her to continue the *Extraordinary Women* series.

Diana arrived from Quadra Island to teach school at Chezacut in a remote corner of the Chilcotin in 1951. Within a year she married local ranch hand and equipment operator Bob French and never left. When Bob got a job driving grader for the Public Works Department in 1957, the young family, which now included two sons, moved to Alexis Creek. Diana spent the next five summers travelling with Bob as he graded the 200-kilometre stretch of Highway 20 between Alexis Creek and Anahim Lake. At first they stayed in the emergency log cabins located strategically along the highway, then Diana kept house in a portable travel trailer with their cat and dog and growing family of boys. They moved camp every three or four days as Bob worked his way along the road.

By the time they moved to Anahim Lake where Bob was posted in 1962, they had four sons and a fifth on the way. They left for Bridge Lake in 1965, then on to Williams Lake in 1970 where Diana has lived ever since.

She says a big motivation behind writing *Women of Brave Mettle* was to acknowledge the lives of women who very quietly went about making a contribution to the community. "A lot of people weren't aware of what they did," she says. "Women haven't had the same spotlight the men have had. Yet in the rough and tumble macho image of the Cariboo Chilcotin, isn't it interesting that Williams Lake has the oldest art society in British Columbia?"

Diana tells the stories of these fifty women as only she can. Candidly, with depth and feeling. Women of distinction, women who made their mark, mothers and daughters, the wives of politicians, the ladies of the *Tribune*, and women gone but not forgotten

She could easily do the stories of a hundred more women, Diana admits. She laments that the allotted space hardly does justice to the lives she portrays. "It's just a snapshot," she says. "Most deserve a whole book written about them."

—*Sage Birchwater*

1

GONE BUT NOT FORGOTTEN

Mickey Dorsey

*T*oday most of the Chilcotin country is served by decent roads, hydro power, television and the Internet. It wasn't always so. The west Chilcotin particularly was a holdout when it came to the trappings of modern civilization. It was a man's country, the last frontier, but some remarkable women lived there.

One of them was Mickey Dorsey. She is best known as a schoolteacher, one of the special kind who can really "make people learn." She had boundless enthusiasm for learning and for life in general, and it was catching. Everyone was better for having known her.

She was born Hannah Clarissa Tuck in 1911 in Sidney, Nova Scotia. Her father was a sea captain and a ship builder, and in 1914 the family came to Vancouver where he managed Western Canada Shipyards. He retired in 1922, when Mickey was eleven, and moved to Bella Coola valley where, among other things, he designed and built boats for local fishermen.

As a child, Mickey watched the pack trains with their strings of horses come and go from the Chilcotin plateau. She listened to tales of the Great Beyond up the mountain, and she dreamed of seeing it for herself. She went to a one-room school in the valley until Grade 8, then to Ocean Falls for high school. When she was home for holidays she made a few trips by horseback with friends to the Rainbow Mountains and the Anahim Lake area. She loved the high country and the adventures encountered getting there by horseback.

After receiving her teaching certificate from the Vancouver Normal School, Mickey spent two years teaching in Port Simpson, near Prince Rupert. She thoroughly enjoyed her time there. The community was sports-minded and so was she. (She was a strong swimmer, once swimming from the Bella Coola wharf to the cannery across the bay, a distance of at least three kilometres.) She and a nurse bought a little speedboat and they went to Prince Rupert on weekends.

When her mother became ill, Mickey went home to care for her, and by the time she was better it was too late to apply for a school. As it happened, former Bella Coola residents Andy and Dorothy Christensen were ranching at the Clesspocket Ranch at Anahim Lake, and they asked Mickey to teach their two young daughters. She was delighted. Getting to Anahim meant three days on saddle horse over the treacherous but spectacular trail up the mountain, but for Mickey that was part of the adventure. She was to make more than a few trips over that trail.

Mickey had met Lester Dorsey, one of the Clesspocket cowboys, at rodeos in the valley. He was handsome, charming, and a true frontiersman. He'd found his way to the Chilcotin country from Washington State and he wasn't as interested in putting down roots as he was in seeing what was around the next bend in the road.

When she wasn't teaching, Mickey spent time with Lester, feeding cattle, riding, trapping and listening to his stories. They decided to marry in the spring and start a ranch of their own. Her family was not delighted about this, but the two wed in March 1934 in Bella Coola.

As it turned out, they were to have several ranches of their own. Lester couldn't settle in one place for long. He'd take up property, get a place started, and as soon as the operation began to prosper, or looked like it might, he'd move on.

Their first ranch, the River Ranch, was on the Dean River. Mickey was taken aback to learn she was to feed a hay crew. She said they would have starved to death if it hadn't been for the Native women who befriended her, and she always credited them for teaching her not only how to cook, but how to survive in the often unforgiving Chilcotin climate. She learned to put up hay, pack horses and deal with all kinds of ranching emergencies. She learned too about wolves, bear and moose, bitter cold weather and loneliness. Her first homes were one-room cabins with dirt roofs, miles from the nearest neighbour.

Son Dave arrived in January 1935. Lester and Mickey rode down to Bella Coola the month before. The weather was cold, the snow deep, and the horses had to break trail. Lester went home, but snowshoed back down when Dave was born. Mickey wasn't well enough to go home until spring when she and Lester rode back up the mountain with Dave in a basket made of willow branches.

Often Mickey would be alone for one reason or another. Lester might be rounding up cattle, on a beef drive, or getting the mail and supplies. He was usually gone longer than expected, leaving Mickey to cope on her own. Coping meant anything from roping a wild cow to get milk for Dave, to pulling cattle and horses from mud holes, feeding them in minus-thirty-degree weather, getting firewood or chopping water holes. She carried buckets of water from the river on a yoke on her shoulders. One cabin had a dirt floor, but most had rough wood planks and she made canvas pants for the crawling babies so they wouldn't get slivers. In her spare time she trapped muskrats and sold the furs.

Their second son Steve was due in November 1936, the year of the big flood in Bella Coola. When Mickey went down in October the road was awash and she made the last part of the trip in a rowboat. Deep snow on the mountain kept her in the valley until spring. She rode home with a pack train carrying farm equipment, with Dave in front of her and Steve in a basket on her back. It was a horrible trip. The horse bucked off their packs and Mickey's back ached from the weight of the basket. Lester had made arrangements to take the machinery to Pan Phillips' ranch on the other side of the Itcha Mountains, so instead of going home they spent the summer there. Mickey was the designated cook.

As a child, Mickey dreamed of the high country on the Chilcotin plateau.

Whatever the circumstances, Mickey saw beauty in her surroundings. On that trip they crossed a glacier at sunset, and she wrote about it in her memoirs: "The whole world seemed to reflect the colours. That night at camp the melody of the horse bells, the music from a little creek, and the seeming closeness of the stars brought me peace and contentment."

She took joy in the cry of a loon, the call of geese, the howl of a wolf or the sight of a caribou silhouetted against an evening sky.

When Lester took up property at Pelican Lake, they divided their time between the two places. When the hay ran out at the River Ranch they took themselves, their belongings, the cattle, horses and sheep across both Anahim and Pelican lakes on the ice. They had some frightful crossings but Mickey didn't worry as long as Lester was in the lead.

When Lester sold the River Ranch to buy more cattle, they moved to Pelican Lake. Their house there was only two kilometres from the Bella Coola Trail and it was a handy stopover for travellers on their way to and from the valley. Everyone was welcome to stay for a day or a week, sharing good conversation and whatever was in the pot for supper. Warm hospitality, laughter and a talent to make long and loyal friendships were a huge part of Mickey's personality.

Third son Mike was born in 1938 at Anahim with the assistance of frontier nurse Jane Bryant. The Bella Coola Trail was too difficult to tackle with three little ones, and the third baby restricted Mickey's visiting. She could ride saddle horse to a neighbour's with two little ones but not with three. Her parents came to stay with her while Lester was on the beef drive that year and her dad built a smokehouse, a rowboat, and made all kinds of improvements to the cabin. Life was good.

Jack was born in 1940. He was a husky baby but he fell ill the winter he was five. Mickey was expecting her fifth baby any day, so Lester took Jack to hospital in Vancouver where he underwent surgery for a brain tumour. Sadly, he didn't survive the operation. Frank was born at Pelican Lake before Lester returned. Years later Frank and his wife, Darlene, gave Mickey a family birthstone ring for Christmas. The first thing she said when she saw it was, "You remembered Jack!"

Mickey shared Lester's itch to see what was on the other side of the mountain, and whenever she had a chance to go somewhere, she went. She made some wonderful trips on saddle horse, including an eight-hundred-kilometre round trip to Vanderhoof.

Before they had married, Lester had owned the Three Circle Ranch. When it came up for sale, he wanted to buy it. Mickey was happy where she was and would have preferred keeping one ranch, but when a hunter offered to buy the Pelican Lake place for a hunting lodge, Lester couldn't resist. Mickey accepted the inevitable. Three Circle was bigger and was on higher ground, but it meant starting all over again in a rough cabin. That was bad enough but Lester suggested she go back to teaching while he went guiding for the new owner of Pelican Lake.

Mickey Dorsey loved the outdoors and, when she wasn't ranching or teaching, spent as much time as she could on horseback or on the water. After retiring she fulfilled a long-time dream and canoed down the Blackwater River.

Mickey had been homeschooling the boys. Now she bundled them up and went to a school at Rose Lake, near Williams Lake. The next year she opened a school at ,Anahim Lake for the Department of Indian Affairs. She took two-year-old Frank to school with her. She drew a chalk line near the back of the schoolroom and told him not to cross it while the children were doing their lessons. He didn't step over the line until it was recess time.

The next year Lester was ready to ranch again and Mickey and the children went back to Three Circle. With a few years of hard work, the ranch was running smoothly. They had a proper house, fences, and a decent cattle herd. They had two more children, Wanda, born in 1951, and Fred in 1953. Mickey taught off and on, and all was well until Lester decided to sell Three Circle and move to the Four Mile Ranch, farther off the beaten track. Mickey was particularly upset this time because he sold the furniture with the house, and it included a cradle and other items her dad had made.

The three older boys were on their own, and Frank was staying with an uncle in Washington going to school. He returned for Grade 9 in Williams Lake, living at the dormitory. When Wanda was ready for high school, Mickey applied for a position in Williams Lake where she rented a condo for herself, Wanda and Fred. Her arrival in Williams Lake was good luck for the principal of Crescent Heights School, who had initiated an open area classroom and needed teachers who knew how to handle multi-grades. Mickey and long-time Williams Lake-area teacher Doreen Armes were a formidable team.

Students of all ages loved Mickey. Nothing fazed her. She had all the patience in the world, and was quick to recognize potential problems. She had time to listen. She got along with everyone without compromising her own principles, and she had a great sense of humour. Most of her own education was acquired outside the classroom but she took numerous university courses to keep up with the times.

Mickey retired in 1976 with no regrets. She loved teaching but she said retirement was a natural part of life. She took time to travel, both locally and abroad. She visited parts of the Chilcotin she hadn't seen before, canoed down the Blackwater River, visited the Queen Charlottes (Haida Gwaii) and went to Mexico and Alaska. She also turned her hand to the arts. She believed creative talents are made for enjoyment, and don't have to be developed to perfection. She enjoyed making pottery, painting, writing and spinning.

Cancer caught up with her eventually. Typically, she didn't give into it without a fight, and she was being flown from Bella Coola for surgery in Vancouver on May 24, 1982, when the small aircraft she was in flipped while taxiing into the bay at Port Hardy. They couldn't get Mickey out in time.

Lester had a hard time accepting her death. He died, quite unexpectedly, of a heart attack less than a month later. They are both buried in the small Anahim Lake cemetery, overlooking the stampede grounds.

Kathleen Telford

Lady Rancher

During her long and busy life, Kathleen Telford was a cowgirl, nurse, wife, widowed mother, rancher, historian, author and community volunteer.

She was born at Hanceville in the Chilcotin Valley in January 1901, the second daughter of Chilcotin pioneers Alex and Anna Graham. Alex arrived in the Chilcotin from Ireland in 1887 and worked on ranches in the Riske Creek area. In 1889, his fiancée, Anna Harvey, travelled from the old country to marry him. In 1891 they partnered with Archie McAuley in establishing the A1 Ranch at Alexis Creek.

Kathleen and her older sister Frances helped with every job on the ranch. They cooked and cleaned, fed the chickens, cleared land, put up hay and rounded up cattle. Kathleen was five when she went on her first roundup. Frances put her on a gentle horse, but she fell behind the other riders. Frances went back to look for her and found her still coming along, but her saddle had turned and she was underneath the horse's belly, hanging on for dear life.

She could and did ride any kind of horse, and she said she was bucked off "in every way imaginable." She had mishaps with the animals when she wasn't riding them too. When she was twelve she was raking hay in a meadow some three and a half kilometres from home when the team bolted. She was thrown off the seat,

Kathleen Telford ended her professional nursing career as nurse and manager of the Red Cross Outpost Hospital at Alexis Creek. She dealt with everything from delivering babies to emergency first aid and dealing with tick bites.

narrowly missing the running horses' hooves, and was scooped up under the teeth of the wildly turning rake along with the hay. The reins tangled, eventually stopping the horses, and Kathleen escaped by prying apart the rake teeth. She was dizzy, but unhurt.

Kathleen and the McAuley girls received their early schooling from a governess, then Kathleen went to All Hallows, an Anglican private school for girls in Yale. The journey was made by horse and buggy with overnight camp-outs along the way. Kathleen stayed at Yale until the school term was over, with no trips home for holidays in between.

After All Hallows, she went to St. Paul's Hospital in Vancouver, receiving her Registered Nurses Certificate in 1925. Her first job was at the Tranquille TB Sanitorium in Kamloops. By then she had a car, and the road to Tranquille was called "the Graham Highway" because she always drove the biggest—and fastest—of cars to and from work.

She met George Telford in Kamloops and they married in 1929. George first worked for Alex, then took over the Grahams' Armstrong Ranch, later called the KC Ranch and now the Canyon Ranch. Along with raising her family, Kathleen cared for her mother, who was an invalid for some years. When any ranch animals were ailing, her nursing skills were called upon.

After receiving her RN from Royal Inland Hospital in Kamloops, Kathleen spent some time nursing at the Tranquille Tuberculosis Sanatorium in the same city.

George died in 1948 of a heart attack, leaving Kathleen with five children, the youngest four years old. She took over running the ranch in a time when there were few women ranch bosses. A 1951 story in a Vancouver newspaper told of Kathleen attending a provincial Red Cross meeting at the Hotel Vancouver.

"Mrs. Kathleen Telford, rancher, looks as if she would be far more at home presiding at a ladies' aid meeting than superintending the branding of cattle."(The writer obviously didn't know about the bronc riding.) The story describes her "wearing a muskrat coat, her auburn hair waving out from under a tiny black hat crested with feathers, her blue eyes smiling behind her glasses, speaking in a soft, faintly Irish voice as she shyly admitted ownership of a 3000-acre ranch at Alexis Creek, 75 miles west of Williams Lake. Widowed in 1948, she took over the 400 head of cattle and now runs the ranch with the help of a 'sort of foreman,' two or three hired men, and 17-year-old-twin sons, Norman and Bill."

Ranching may have been a man's world, but Kathleen knew a quality cow or bull when she saw one, as cattlemen bidding against her at cattle sales soon found out. Her young steers frequently won trophies. The ranchers, with respect, called her "Cattle Kate."

In the late fifties, Kathleen divided the ranch between her three sons, and took the position of nurse at the Red Cross Outpost Hospital at Alexis Creek. She delivered babies, provided emergency first aid for serious accidents, and handled whatever came her way with calm good humour. Youngsters called her "Nurse Granny." She went back to ranching when youngest son Bob finished high school.

In 1969 she retired to Williams Lake where she became very active in the Old Age Pensioners Organization (OAPO), serving for many years as president. She enjoyed travelling and made trips to the South Pacific, Ireland, England and Alaska. She was one of the first *Tribune* newspaper correspondents and for many years wrote the news of the Chilcotin country. When she moved to town, she wrote the OAPO news and stories of her travelling adventures. She had a keen interest in the history of the Cariboo, particularly the Chilcotin, and she wrote a manuscript that unfortunately was lost when her home at Alexis Creek burned in the early 1960s. Excerpts from the book were published during the BC Centennial and later in *BC Outdoors*. She painstakingly re-wrote the manuscript but it has not been published. Oddly enough, while her writing detailed the history of her family and other pioneers, she was strangely reticent about her personal history. She died at home in Williams Lake in 1982 at the age of eighty-one.

Kathleen grew up on her parents' ranch at Alexis Creek where she cooked for ranch crews and rounded up cattle on horseback.

Daughters Louise and Olive didn't stay in the Cariboo, but the twins and Bob did. Bill and Bob left ranching for other interests, and Norman and his family stayed on the home ranch. Norman passed away in 2003. His wife, Valerie, remains on the ranch, which is now managed by daughter Bev and her husband, Al Madley. Their son, Garret, is the fifth generation on the ranch, which has been in the family for over one hundred years.

Jessie Pigeon

The First Female Government Agent

*J*essie Foster Pigeon went where no woman had gone before—she was the first woman in British Columbia (if not Canada) to serve as government agent and gold commissioner. She was also district registrar of the Supreme Court. It was a man's world, but according to all reports, she did the three jobs efficiently and with good humour for seventeen years.

Jessie was born in Quesnel in 1904 to a pioneer family. Her maternal grandfather was Robert McLeese, who came to the Cariboo in 1863 in the balmy days of the gold rush. He established a ranch and a stopping place at Soda Creek, located between Quesnel and Williams Lake. He was postmaster there for years. He also represented the Cariboo in the legislative assembly of British Columbia from 1882 to 1888. McLeese Lake was named in his honour.

Jessie's mother, Jean, was the first white child born at Soda Creek. Her dad, Captain Donald Foster, skippered the paddlewheelers that plied the upper Fraser River between Soda Creek and Prince George carrying freight and passengers. Jessie and her sister Linda went to school in Quesnel.

She began her career with the BC government in 1927 as a clerk in the Williams Lake office. Ten years later she was appointed deputy district registrar, working under

L.C. Mclure. When he retired in 1942, she applied for and was named to the top jobs. At the time, there were very few women in the BC government service, none holding responsible positions. The government agent is a top regional civil-service position that dates back to gold rush days. Agents were multi-purpose administrators, responsible for a wide range of provincial services including land registration, collecting taxes, and registering births and marriages. There were so few provincial ministries in the 1940s that Jessie was the go-to person for almost anything that came along involving provincial matters, from trivial complaints to complicated land disputes.

As district registrar she was involved in a wide variety of court cases, divorces, murders, and everything in between. The courthouse was in downtown Williams Lake on the main street, and it was often noisy, especially at stampede times. For years she was the only woman in the building, but she worked with the lawyers and judges on an equal footing.

It was a man's world, but she worked on equal footing...

The job she liked best was that of gold commissioner. Although the Cariboo gold rush was long over in the 1940s and '50s, the lust for gold wasn't. Jessie had to examine claims on location and that took her out of the office and out into the hinterlands. When she could, she drove to sites in her convertible car, but some jobs required travelling by horseback. The weather didn't always cooperate. Once she rode saddle horse for sixty-five kilometres over Snowshoe Plateau from Keithley Creek to Barkerville. It was a rough trip at the best of times but on the way home, she and her guide, former Hudson's Bay Factor Ray Hamilton, were caught in a blizzard on the mountain. Hamilton brought them home safely but Jessie said it wasn't a trip she'd care to repeat.

Jessie met some fascinating people. Many of the prospectors were lonely bachelors who devoted their lives to looking for gold, but there were also business magnates, such as millionaire James Dole, the Pineapple King. He spread blueprints all over her office floor and crawled around on his hands and knees to look at them.

Jessie started the local Girls Guides in 1934, and was the first captain of the Williams Lake Girl Guide Company. The first summer she and assistant Laura Moxon took ten guides on a ten-day camp-out at a remote lake in the Chilcotin. They travelled to and from the lake in the back of a cattle truck, camped in canvas tents and slept on pine tree boughs.

In 1956 Jessie married Leslie Pigeon, a member of a pioneer Cariboo family. Les was a partner in the Western, Rife and Pigeon grocery store in Williams Lake. Jessie retired in 1959 after thirty-two years in the government service. In 1965 Leslie retired from the store, and the two moved to the Alkali Lake Ranch where they operated the ranch's general store. Jessie organized a Brownies' group at the neighbouring Alkali Lake First Nations village.

In 1971 the province built a new modern courthouse in Williams Lake, and Jessie was given the honour of cutting the ribbon at the official opening.

The Pigeons retired from the store business and moved to Vancouver in 1976. When Les died in 1981, Jessie returned to Williams Lake. She lived at Cariboo Park Home until health problems took her to extended care in Prince George. She died there in 1986 at eighty-two years old.

Image on page 22: Former Government Agent Jessie Pigeon was on hand in 1971 to officially open the new courthouse building in Williams Lake with Premier W.A.C. Bennett.

Jane Lehman

She was known as BC's Frontier Florence Nightingale, and rightfully so. For almost forty years she provided health care to the residents of BC's last frontier—the vast, wild, barely populated west Chilcotin country. For many of those years she was the only medical practitioner in the area and she covered it by saddle horse. Her name was Jane Bryant Lehman.

Although she shunned the limelight, tales of her accomplishments have been told in several books, and her dedication to her profession was recognized posthumously in 1988 with the International Red Cross Florence Nightingale award for outstanding service.

Jane was born in Absartee, Montana, on March 31, 1913, the eldest of Cyrus and Phyllis Bryant's four children. The family came to British Columbia in 1919, settling at Soda Creek in the east Chilcotin. They later went to Riske Creek to work for Fred Becher, who had a stopping place, stables and a ranch with cattle and sheep. Phyllis was the cook, and Cyrus tended the horses. Jane, who at nine was an accomplished horsewoman, was the sheepherder. She was a conscientious worker and never lost an animal in her care. She made good use of the Bryants' lone saddle horse. There was a bounty on coyotes, and with brother Alfred, seven, riding behind her saddle, she chased and caught them to make a few dollars.

In 1924 Cyrus found a place at Tatla Lake in the west Chilcotin. He built a cabin there, but with one thing and another it was December before the family was ready to move. They were hardly on the road when the temperature dropped to minus thirty. Cyrus drove their large covered wagon pulled by four horses. Along with their household goods and vegetables, it held Phyllis's precious Heintzman piano. A friend drove a smaller wagon, and Phyllis and the youngest daughter, Bunch, had a buckboard. Jane, Alfred and Caroline rode saddle horse (or walked to keep warm) driving the few head of cattle. It was a hideous trip. They camped most nights, but one night they stayed overnight at Lee's Corner. Cyrus left a kerosene lamp burning in the wagon to keep the supplies from freezing. It tipped over in the night starting a fire that burned the wagon and everything in it. Neighbouring ranchers pitched

Frontier nurse Jane Bryant Lehman was one of the few to receive the Florence Nightingale medal, the highest international distinction that can be awarded to a nurse.

in with clothes and food, and the Bryants continued the trip, arriving at Tatla Lake the day before Christmas.

They were there for nine years, and times were difficult for them during the Depression. Jane had her sights set on a medical career. She wanted to be a doctor, but that was beyond her reach. She practised nursing on anything and everything, including her young siblings. Alfred later said they got tired of that after awhile.

The Tatla school ended at Grade 8 so Phyllis took the children to Williams Lake to continue their education. She worked in a dry goods store, then opened a confectionery, and she played the piano with local bands. The older children worked whenever and wherever they could. The Williams Lake school ended at Grade 10, so Jane went to North Vancouver for Grade 11, working for her board. She took her first year nurses' training at Royal Inland Hospital and her Grade 12 at the same time.

In the meantime, Cyrus moved to Anahim Lake to start another ranch, taking Alfred and Caroline with him. Phyllis and Bunch stayed in Williams Lake for a few more years. After graduation, Jane worked at the Tranquille Sanitorium in Kamloops for a time before joining the family at Anahim.

A tall, willowy young woman, Jane was also a determined one, and she soon put her nurse's training to use. She saw a need for health care among the First Nations, and she set about providing it. The west Chilcotin was sparsely populated. Roads, even wagon roads, were all but non-existent. Jane rode saddle horse over lonely bush trails with whatever medical supplies she had in a backpack. It was a long day's ride from Anahim to the Ulkatcho village, but for the trips to the Blackwater country she took a pack horse and camped overnight. She had some scares. Once some wolves followed her, but she kept a steady pace, and they eventually lost interest in her. She visited each village once a month in every season. Nothing stopped her; no weather was too brutal, no circumstance too difficult.

For two years her only remuneration was the gratitude of her patients. A challenging experience with Ulkatcho Chief Domas Squinas finally convinced her to ask for outside help. The chief was gored by a moose, and his wounds were deep and dirty. After using a pair of wire pliers as forceps, pulling grass, leaves and twigs from his wounds and sewing them up with a sewing needle and horse hair, Jane wrote to the Red Cross asking for a few instruments, such as proper needles. The Red Cross obliged, and at one point hoped to establish an outpost hospital in the area, but that didn't happen. When word of her work reached the outside world she got a small grant from the province and a donation of $56 from Bella Coola residents. She used the money to buy medical supplies.

First Nations health care was, and still is, the responsibility of the Federal Department of Indian Affairs, and when department officials finally found out what Jane was doing, they provided her with medical supplies, some drugs and later a salary. She worked for the federal health ministry from 1937 to 1955. If she ever missed a trip to the reservations during that time, no one remembers it.

The First Nations were her first concern, but Jane looked after everyone who needed her and she never refused a call for help. There was hardly a person living in the west Chilcotin at that time who wasn't on the receiving end of her care. She attended every kind of situation: nursing the ill, setting broken bones, stitching wounds, delivering babies and giving shots. She saved more than a few lives, and she didn't let personal problems interfere with her work. Once she rode with a broken foot to see a patient. Her family tried to talk her out of going but she said she didn't need her foot to ride. It never did heal properly.

Her nursing skills were legendary. She coped with situations that would have daunted a doctor, and she learned to improvise because she had to. Bella Coola was the centre for trade, medical services and the Indian agency. Getting there from Anahim meant a long ride down the mountain. Jane made many trips with patients, sometimes with Cyrus and Alfred, who had a packing business between the two communities, and sometimes on her own. Once she made the trip with a sick baby in her arms.

The annual stampede was Anahim Lake's big event, and Jane was always on hand to tend to cowboys who got themselves injured. At one stampede she caught the eye of Bill Lehman, a cowboy from Chezacut. He left his job there and found one at Anahim so he could court her. They were married in 1941.

The arrival of twin babies didn't stop Jane's trips to the reserves. Her brother Alfred told the story of how when they were tiny the little ones rode in baskets, one on each side of the pack horse. When they were older they rode with her, "one before and one behind."

Jane died on December 1, 1983, in Williams Lake. Although she'd refused all publicity (she considered it an intrusion into her private life) fellow nurses in the Cariboo were well aware of her work, and they nominated her for the Florence Nightingale medal, which was awarded posthumously. The medal is the highest international distinction that can be awarded a nurse. It recognizes exceptional courage and devotion to duty, exemplary services or a creative and pioneering spirit in the areas of public health. Jane qualified on all counts.

Anne Stevenson

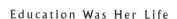

Education Was Her Life

Anne Mackenzie Stevenson was small in stature, but large in spirit. She was a wife and mother, educator, trailblazer, historian, collector of antiquities, adviser to many groups and individuals and a hostess of renown. She had incredible energy and the ability to stir people to action, and she did it all with a twinkle in her eye.

Although she was the daughter of Williams Lake pioneers, and she herself became one of the community's leading citizens, Anne didn't actually live in the town until 1948. Her Scottish parents, Roderick and Elizabeth Mackenzie, were living in Johannesburg, South Africa, when Anne was born in 1903. In 1909 the family immigrated to Canada, settling in Squamish where Roderick had a wholesale dry goods business. In 1919, when he learned the Pacific Great Eastern Railway was being extended and that Williams Lake would become BC's major cattle shipping centre, he made his way north and established the first general store in the new village. It was located on Railway (Mackenzie) Avenue. He was one of the community's foremost citizens, serving on many local organizations, and he was the Cariboo's member of the legislature for ten years.

Anne was still at school in 1919 and she stayed in Vancouver to finish her education, coming "home" to Williams Lake for holidays. She planned to go into

Anne Mackenzie Stevenson was a tireless community worker who was just as much at home playing the organ at church as she was entertaining important people at parties, but she devoted much of her time and energy to working in education.

nursing, but her health wasn't up to it so she switched to history and English at the University of British Columbia. At the time, few women graduated from high school, and even fewer attended university.

The UBC campus was a collection of ragtag buildings, and in 1922 Anne joined a group who walked from downtown Vancouver to the Point Grey campus to lobby for proper facilities. In 1986, UBC's Alma Mater Society presented her with a Great Trekker Award, and she made a symbolic trek at age eighty-three. The award is presented to UBC alumni who achieve eminence in their chosen activity, make a worthy contribution to their community, and take a keen interest in UBC undergrad and graduate students.

Williams Lake was, and still is, the centre for Cariboo Chilcotin ranching communities, and the annual stampede was the main event. On her visits home Anne participated in community events, and that included riding in the stampede parade as a hurdy-gurdy girl. Later in life she was given an honourary lifetime membership in the Stampede Association.

The village had a tennis club but few women members, so Anne played men's singles or made a fourth in men's doubles. She did well enough to qualify for the UBC tennis finals one year. Following her graduation in 1927 with a BA and a teaching certificate, Anne toured Europe. On her return she accepted a post teaching high school English in Kamloops. At barely five feet tall, she was often mistaken for a student.

In 1932, Anne married Doug Stevenson. The two met at UBC where Doug was an engineering student. They belonged to the university's outdoors club and discovered that along with a love of the outdoors, they shared an interest in books, history, antiques, and each other. Their wedding, held at Williams Lake's Stampede

Hall, was the Cariboo's social event of the decade. Roderick announced the nuptials on the front page of the *Tribune* newspaper, inviting everyone to the festivities. Everyone accepted. Anne's wedding dress is now on display at the Museum of the Cariboo Chilcotin.

The newlyweds lived in Trail where Doug worked for Cominco, but within a year he was transferred to a tiny mining town in northern Ontario. There was no accommodation there for Anne so she returned to Williams Lake. After a few months she wrote to Doug saying she wanted to join him. She was on her way east before he had time to answer. For a time they lived in what Anne called a "hovel." She was the only woman there and few of the miners spoke English. To keep busy she worked in the cookhouse with the French-Canadian cook. He taught her to make a pea soup that became her specialty for feeding family and guests.

The Stevensons spent twelve years in Ontario and Quebec, and their three daughters, Elizabeth, Rhona and Jean, were born there. Anne was a full-time mother, as women's liberation was unheard of in the 1930s and married women weren't allowed to teach. Single women were paid less than men. Once, when a teacher left the school, Anne filled in, but only after some argument, and she was paid the lesser wage. She donated her earnings to establish a Girl Guides group.

The Stevensons came back to BC in 1946 when Doug became manager of the Cariboo Gold Quartz Mine in Wells. They lived there until 1948 when they moved to Williams Lake and Doug managed the hardware department at Mackenzie's Store.

Anne became very involved in the local education scene, and her first role saw her promoting a referendum to raise funds for a new high school. She campaigned not only for the school, but for a dormitory for students who lived too far away to make a daily commute to the school. She resumed her teaching career more or less by accident. Daughter Jean came home one morning because her teacher was away and there were no substitutes. Anne decided to try teaching elementary classes and she was soon subbing on a regular basis.

Then she ran for and was elected as a trustee on the Williams Lake and District School Board (School District #27). She served one year before returning to the classroom to teach English and history to Grades 9 to 12 at Williams Lake Junior/Senior High School. She was one of the few teachers in the Cariboo with a university degree. She was girls' counsellor, head of the English Department and taught drama on the side. Her drama students won prizes in Prince George and Kamloops.

Anne retired from teaching in 1965 but not from education; she simply switched lanes. She was elected again as a trustee for School District #27. She served on the board for ten years, two as the district's first woman chair. She had a good sense of humour and was a team player, but as a chairperson she didn't hesitate to lay down the law when required. While on the board, she was instrumental in introducing new curricula to the district, including programs preserving First Nations culture and language. When a new school was built, her fellow trustees named it the Anne Stevenson Junior Secondary School in her honour.

Anne's thinking on education was far ahead of the times. While she believed education was necessary for a happy and productive life, she wasn't overly concerned when students dropped out of school. The key, she believed, was to make sure the doors were open for them to drop back in. She believed students should get as much schooling as possible in their home communities, and to that end she campaigned to bring post-secondary education to Williams Lake.

District #27 was one of five districts in the BC School Trustees Association's Cariboo Mainland branch. Along with chairing the branch and serving on a number of committees, Anne founded a regional group that lobbied the Minister of Education for a regional post-secondary institution. Their efforts were rewarded in 1970 when Cariboo College was established in Kamloops. Anne chaired the college council and received an honourary membership on the council when she retired ten years later.

While on the college council she lobbied for a Williams Lake campus, and it became a reality in 1972. In 1978 the campus was recognized under the BC Colleges and Institutes Act. It moved to a building on Hodgson Road in 1989. In 1995 it became the University College of the Cariboo, and in March 2004 it became the Williams Lake campus of Thompson Rivers University (TRU). Anne didn't live to see this dream come true, but TRU is housed in the former Anne Stevenson Junior Secondary School building. A plaque commemorating her role is prominently displayed.

Anne's interests weren't limited to education. She undertook every cause with enthusiasm, charm and determination, whether it was chairing a prestigious organization or helping with tedious volunteer work. She took an active part in the local Museum Society, the Library Association, and Union Board of Health. She found time to play the organ at St. Andrew's United Church on Sundays, and she and Doug were major contributors to 4H. She was the first chair of the BC Sites Advisory Committee, and was on the first board of Simon Fraser University. She and Doug were founding members of the SFU Convocation ceremony, and she received an honourary Doctor of Laws from the university in 1982. The Stevensons were active members of the BC Historical Association; Anne was president of the group for six years then named honourary president. In 1983 she received a lifetime membership.

The Stevensons' interest in BC history led them to be collectors, and their stately home, located on the shores of Williams Lake, surpassed many community museums in terms of artifacts and archives. Their First Nations collection was priceless. One treasure was a grizzly bear mantlepiece in red cedar, carved for them in 1954 by noted carver Bill Reid. It was one of his first big pieces. The unique carving was donated to the Royal BC Museum and Government House in Victoria. It now hangs over a fireplace in Government House.

In the early years of their marriage, Anne and Doug often went without other things so they could buy books, and over the years they built up an impressive library of historical books and documents. Their collection of Pacific Northwest Coast history first editions was believed to be the best in the province and many noted historians visited their home to study them. When they sold Mackenzie's Store in 1968, Doug and Anne toured the Orient for two months and came home with a magnificent collection of Oriental art and pottery.

The Stevensons were Williams Lake's unofficial hosts on many occasions as they made their home available for events ranging from soirees for visiting dignitaries to huge receptions such as the city's golden jubilee celebrations. They welcomed the numerous authors, politicians, scholars, historians and researchers who came to visit. The Mackenzies had always held an open house on New Year's Day (Hogmanay in Scotland) and Doug and Anne continued the tradition until Doug's death in 1973. It wasn't unusual for as many as two hundred guests to attend. Anne always cooked a tremendous roast beef for the event.

Anne's nine grandchildren called her "Annemum." When Annemum celebrated her eightieth birthday, her family hosted a party that saw hundreds of guests come to wish her well.

She spent her last years in a seniors' residence in Coquitlam where she was a favourite among both residents and staff. She died on August 6, 1995, one month before her ninety-second birthday. A well-attended remembrance service was held in Williams Lake that September.

Lily Kozuki

All's Well That Ends Well

Like many pioneers, Lily Kozuki left a cozy home and comfortable lifestyle in the city for a shack in the bush, but there were some big differences. Far from being willing pioneers, the Kozukis were forced into exile, and they were not welcomed in the Cariboo.

Lily's world began turning upside down in December 1941 when Japanese aircraft bombed the US naval base at Pearl Harbor, Hawaii. The Kozukis were appalled by the attack, but they didn't expect any trouble because they were Canadian citizens. They were wrong. Fearing a Japanese naval attack on the BC coast, the Canadian government treated all Japanese in BC as enemies, regardless of citizenship, and made them leave their homes in coastal communities.

Tiny, bright-eyed, and always busy, Lily Masako Yasuda was born in 1906 and raised in Vancouver, the daughter of a well-to-do commercial fisherman. Her parents were proud Canadians who taught her to appreciate the democratic principles of freedom and fairness. Lily met Fred Kozuki through a mutual friend. It was love at first sight, and they married in 1935. Following a honeymoon in Japan, they returned to live in the gracious five-bedroom Kozuki home in Mt. Pleasant, a middle-class neighbourhood close to Fred's fish and green-grocer's shop. They were the only Japanese family in the area. Fred's father (Fred Sr.) and brother Harry had a landscaping business. All were Canadian citizens.

By 1941, three little ones, Ed, Dick and Freda, had joined the family. Lily had every modern convenience, but she had her hands full looking after the family of seven and keeping an eye on her parents. Fred's mother was in Hiroshima, Japan, caring for her aging parents.

The Brown Place, an abandoned farm on the outskirts of the village of Williams Lake was a far cry from the gracious Kozuki family home in Vancouver. The Kozukis were among the Japanese families forced by the Government of Canada to leave BC coastal communities after war broke out with Japan in 1941.

In January 1942, an RCMP officer knocked on the Kozukis' door and told them to surrender their vehicles, close their businesses, dispose of their home, and be ready to leave for an internment camp on twenty-four-hours' notice. Although they were sure this was all a big mistake, Fred sold the store for practically nothing, and Fred Sr. sold his landscaping tools and arranged to rent the house to a Mr. and Mrs. Watson.

Lily's parents were to be interned in Slocan, BC, but Fred had other ideas. Armed with a statement of his finances and a letter of support from George Luscombe, a former provincial policeman and school chum who lived in Williams Lake, he convinced the authorities to let the family go there instead of to a camp. Relatives and friends thought he was crazy, but he didn't want the children raised in an internment camp. Neither did Lily, but she wasn't overjoyed about going off on their own either. The family wouldn't really be free in Williams Lake. They had to report regularly to the police, they couldn't have guns or radios or leave the area, and they could never, ever, ask for government help.

In June they were given four days to leave Vancouver. They loaded their pickup truck with a wood stove, furniture, food and everything else they could cram into it. Lily left precious family belongings and keepsakes in a locked trunk in a bedroom. Many tears went into the trunk with the treasures, and when she left the house for the last time she couldn't bear to look back. She didn't want a new life. She was happy with the one she had.

Harry drove the truck to Williams Lake, and the others travelled by train. Luscombe had arranged for them to rent a 240-acre farm, the Brown Place, about

The last formal picture taken of Lily Kozuki with her children, Dick, Ed and Freda, before they came to the Cariboo.

ten kilometres from the village of Williams Lake. He'd warned them the place was rustic, but Lily was expecting a proper farm, not dilapidated buildings surrounded by forest and bush. There was a barn, a shack, an outhouse and a well with no pump. The main house, a wee, two-room cabin, had no sink and no cupboards, just a built-in table under a flyspecked window and cracked linoleum on the floor. It was occupied by spiders and pack rats. Lily was dismayed, to put it mildly.

Fred Sr. and Harry moved into the shack. Determined to make the best of it, Lily set about scrubbing the cabin. By the second day her chest was aching and she'd drained the well. The well never did recover, and from then on the men had to haul water from the village in forty-five-gallon drums.

Tribune newspaper publisher George Renner's editorials set the tone for the community's attitude. Among other things, he called the Kozukis coyotes and said they'd sabotage the bridge and the telephone line to the Chilcotin.

Sabotage was the last thing on their minds. They were too busy trying to survive. They knew nothing about animals but they bought a milk cow and chickens, and they cleared land for a big garden. Fred thought that as long as they had food they'd be okay. Lily learned how to cook on a wood stove, make bread, wash clothes on a scrub board, and chase away chicken hawks. The shortage of water was a nightmare for her. She recycled every drop, washing the children, the clothes, then the floor before throwing what water was left on the garden.

When the men got a job for a few weeks putting up hay for a rancher, Lily was left alone with the children. She was terrified. She was sure there were beasts lurking in the bush. The road to the Chilcotin country went by their house and there wasn't much traffic on it, but when she was outside, one trucker shook his fist and yelled racist slurs at her when he went by. She was afraid he'd stop.

The family had just gotten used to the scorching hot Cariboo summer when an early frost flattened the garden, leaving only the root vegetables. By spring everyone

Lily's city clothes weren't too appropriate for life at the Brown Place, but they were all she had, and her stylish hat did the job of protecting her from the hot Cariboo sun as she washed clothes on a scrub board on the cabin porch.

was sick of turnips even though Lily found innovative ways to cook them. Meat was hard to come by. She was sure deer came by and laughed at her because they knew they were safe. Fred Sr. trapped a porcupine once but no one would eat it.

When cold weather froze the water in the drums they melted snow in a copper tub over an outside fire. The wood stove that threw too much heat in summertime couldn't keep them warm in winter. Washing clothes in the tiny cabin was a chore, and water in a bucket beside the stove froze overnight. When the temperature dropped to minus forty and stayed there for days, it caught them without supplies. The truck wouldn't start so Fred walked to the village. He nearly didn't make it.

Cooped up in the small dark cabin for weeks on end, Lily thought winter would never end. She had no female companionship, no one to give her advice. She worried about her parents and Mother Kozuki, but she was still so sure the government would let them go home she hadn't even unpacked everything.

Their savings dwindled and there were no jobs. Luscombe suggested they try selling wood. The landlord agreed, so they bought crosscut saws and set about cutting trees, Harry and Fred Sr. on one saw, Lily and Fred on the other. It was backbreaking work. The snow was knee deep and the saws were longer than the Kozukis were tall. They persevered, but few people bought their wood, and some would take the wood but not pay their bill. Others just helped themselves. The Kozukis didn't

After WWII was over, people eventually got over their prejudices and Lily took her rightful place in the community where she was both loved and respected by all who knew her.

dare raise a fuss about anything. When Lily went to the hospital for her son Roy's birth, she saw a pile of wood outside the hospital window and knew it was theirs by the uneven cuts. That made her mad. Sale of the wood would have paid the eighteen-dollar hospital fee and then some.

That was bad enough but the *Tribune* didn't publish the news of Roy's birth, nor of the later arrivals of Frank and Betty. Of all the slights, this hurt Lily the most. "They published all the other births. It was as though my babies didn't matter," she said.

A few people were friendly, including neighbouring ranchers Jerry and Barbara Buckley, government agent Jessie Foster and general store owner Roderick Mackenzie.

The second summer was easier. The men got a few jobs, although some employers were slow paying them. On the downside, the government sold their Vancouver house. Fred Sr. was paid six hundred dollars for the six-thousand-dollar home. The Watsons sent Lily's trunk but it held only her wedding picture and gown.

Ed was school-age their second fall, so that meant moving closer to the village. Landlords weren't enthusiastic about renting to a big family, especially a big Japanese family, but finally resident George Abbey rented them what Lily considered to be a real house. It had bedrooms and a kitchen and there was a well with water in it. They could grow a good garden, and the property was beside the lake so Fred Sr. could fish. Money was still tight but Lily canned and preserved everything, and her treadle sewing machine worked overtime as she mended and patched clothes, sometimes mending the patches.

Renner continued the hostile editorials, and the school board held a special meeting to vote if Ed should be allowed to go to school (they decided he could) but life did improve. The United Church welcomed them and people soon realized they weren't anybody's enemies. Lily made friends, the men got more work, and Fred developed a construction business.

In 1945 the government let Lily visit her parents in Slocan. She found them living in a tarpaper shack that was worse than the cabin at the Brown Place. It was the last time she saw them. After the war, Japanese evacuees could either return to Japan or relocate east of the Rockies. The Tasudas and Fred Sr. went back to Japan. Fred, Lily and Harry ignored the notices, hoping the government would forget about them, and it did. Even Renner mellowed once the war was over.

When the restrictions were lifted, Fred and Lily bought the Abbey property, but Fred was restless. He'd "worked like a squirrel" but wasn't getting ahead. In 1947 he cashed his life insurance policy and bought a store in Lillooet, leaving the family behind until he was settled. He never did get settled. The store was a disaster.

By then Harry was on his own. The older children helped Lily with the chores. It was a long walk to the village, so she bought her groceries at Overwaitea, the closest store. Roderick Mackenzie arrived on her doorstep one day asking why she'd stopped shopping at his store. When she explained, he said he'd give her a ride home if she returned.

In the spring, the children came down with flu. When eighteen-month-old Betty didn't get better, Lily carried her the two and a half kilometres to the doctor, who gave her medicine and sent her home. Betty died that night in Lily's arms.

That was rock bottom. Fred came home, although he had no job and no prospects. The Buckleys had a motel in the village, and they suggested the Kozukis go into that business. Reluctant at first, Fred reactivated the construction company, borrowed money and built a duplex beside the house. The Lakeside Motel opened in the spring of 1950. Lily ran the motel, and the children were the cleaning crew. The units were clean and comfortable and Lily provided wonderful service. Williams Lake was booming, and the business flourished. After building more units (Lily called a halt at ten) Fred retired from construction.

Although things were going well, the heartaches weren't over. In 1967, days before his wedding, son Frank was killed in a tragic motor vehicle accident.

The story does have a happy ending. After twenty years at the motel, Lily and Fred retired. They spent the next years enjoying their family and friends and travelling all over North America and abroad. They laughed about their troubles in the early days and held no grudges, not even against Mr. Renner. The family says Lily never did stop mending things, and no one will eat turnips. As bad as it had been, Lily said there was never a time when they didn't have food on the table or presents under the Christmas tree. She and Fred had no regrets about coming to the Cariboo.

The affection Williams Lakers held for Lily and Fred was evident with the large number of people who came to pay their respects at their fiftieth and sixtieth wedding anniversary celebrations, and later, at their funerals. Fred passed away in July 2000, Lily in August 2008 at the age of ninety-four.

Lil Deschene

A Woman of Strong Faith and Strong Opinions

*L*ong-time Williams Lake resident Lil Deschene had such a wide range of interests it would take less space to tell what she didn't do than to tell what she did. She was a woman of strong faith, varied interests and strong opinions. She would launch herself wholeheartedly into causes that included—but were not limited to—religion, the arts, music, sports groups, parks and recreation, politics and gardening, and her hand was always out to those who needed help or encouragement.

Lilian Doris Goffin was born November 8, 1919, in Brockley, England. She came to Canada with her mother and sister when she was four. They spent Christmas at sea, and New Year's on the train coming across the country to North Vancouver where her father waited for them.

In 1930 Mr. Goffin caught the homesteading bug and the family moved to Hawkins Lake, near Forest Grove, in the Cariboo. They lived in a tent until mid-December when he finished building their log home. Lil attended school at Bradley Creek.

In 1938 she married Ed Deschene. Originally from Midland, Ontario, where his family's work centered around the Great Lakes' docks, Ed began working on freighters at age thirteen. His family moved west in the 1930s and they settled at Eagle Creek, in the Goffins' neighbourhood. Ed had jobs at mills and ranches until 1940 when he took Lil and small son Al back to Ontario where he worked first in the shipyards, and later on the Great Lakes.

In 1943 the family moved back to the Cariboo. Ed arrived in Williams Lake at 10 a.m. one morning and had a job by afternoon. When Stan Goad, Round House foreman for the Pacific Great Eastern Railway, learned Ed knew something about steam engines, he offered him a job. Ed ended up working thirty-four years with the railway. The job had ups and downs, the work was steady and the pay decent but Ed was away from home twice a week, more if there was a derailment or a snow slide.

Lil Deschene loved her little green house by the railroad tracks in Williams Lake. She lived there from 1943 until she died in 2002.

The railway yard was a tiny subdivision of Williams Lake. Along with the passenger station, Round House and water tower, there were bunkhouses and several homes for employees. Ed and Lil leased a little green house on the wrong side of the tracks that had been built for the station master. The house was close to the railroad tracks but Lil loved living there especially in the days of the steam trains. She said the whistles made a wonderful noise.

The green house wasn't much of a house as houses go, but it was a home with a capital H. For years, under the Deschene open-door (and open-heart) policy, it was a home away from home for priests, teachers, bankers, railway workers, off-duty airmen from the Puntzi Mountain air base, immigrants, strays, and the occasional horse. High ranking politicians and at least one bishop found their way across the railroad tracks. Everyone was welcomed, fed and cared for.

When the four children, Al, Roseanne, Bonnie (Yvonne) and Theresa were growing up, the Deschene home was the gathering place for young people. Lil took an active part in Scouts, Girl Guides, music festivals, the parent-teachers association and every other group that called for parent participation. She made costumes for skating carnivals on an old treadle sewing machine. She and Ed sold hundreds of hamburgers and hot dogs at fundraisers and helped with stampede floats for the Scouts and Brownies. Occasionally her enthusiasm for supporting causes embarrassed the family. They didn't care for the time she slept in the Mackenzie's Store show window dressed in her pajamas after being put to "sleep" by hypnotist Raveen as a promo for his show.

When the Puntzi air base was established in the Chilcotin in the 1950s, many young American servicemen were stationed there. There wasn't much for them to do when they came to Williams Lake on leave. Lil felt sorry for the first batch she came across and took them home. The word got around and the Deschenes' became their in-town destination. Theresa was at the bus depot one day and heard a fellow talking about the Deschenes' great food and hospitality. He thought it was a public facility. Another time Bonnie came home to find a party in full roar. A young airman met her at the door and told her she couldn't come in because the house was full.

Lil did nothing by halves. Ed was a Roman Catholic and Lil converted when they married, soon becoming a pillar of the church. When they moved to Williams Lake she did the altar, preparing the linens and flowers. She belonged to the Catholic Women's League, sang in the choir and mother-henned the priests. The girls remember being towed to church on a toboggan in the winter. Al was an altar boy.

Christmas was a special occasion at the Deschenes'. On Christmas Day, Lil and Ed would look for people who were alone and invite them home for dinner. Guests and family sat at a table made up of blanket-covered boards sitting on buckets of frozen sawdust. The gatherings eventually became international dinners after Christmas when guests brought a favourite ethnic dish and a friend. Lil delighted in entertaining any time of year. Her St. Patrick's Day dinners were a treat. Everyone wore green clothes and ate green food.

Lil Deschene did nothing by halves.

Lil was a strong advocate of the arts. She had a lovely voice and along with singing in choirs she enjoyed participating in musical theatre, such as Gwen Ringwood's *The Road Runs North*. She was interested in sports and recreation and was a member of Williams Lake's 1971 Centennial Committee that established Boitanio Park. During her lifetime she defended the park and woe betide anyone who had what she considered nefarious designs on it. She was a champion for the river valley long before many Williams Lakers realized it was there, and was one of the first to recycle and campaign against noxious chemicals such as DDT. For years she participated in fall fairs. She was a Lady of the Royal Purple and a long-time supporter and canvasser for both the cancer and arthritis societies. She volunteered for the National Institute for the Blind for eighteen years, and she was involved in establishing both Cariboo Park Home and Cariboo Lodge. She was a founding member of the original museum and historical society, and a lifetime member of the current one. She was also one of the first members of the local credit union.

She not only took part in activities, she wrote about them. Along with writing letters to support various projects (or not) she was a correspondent for the *Williams Lake Tribune*, the *Quesnel Observer*, the *BC Catholic* and the now defunct *Kamloops Sentinel*. She began her career in journalism by submitting poetry to the *Tribune* (she also established its first paper route). After Clive Stangoe bought the paper, she covered a Pacific Great Eastern Railway derailment and that led to a long-time relationship with the Stangoes. She was also an accomplished photographer. She kept things, like back issues of newspapers, and this turned out to be a boon for the museum, which has a significant Deschene collection of both photos and artifacts. She often wrote comments on margins of newspaper stories, some a bit caustic.

The Deschenes grew a large garden. Lil's favourite flower was the yellow rose. When they first moved to the railway property Lil planted some lilac sprigs and they grew to enormous proportions. Rhubarb and flowers transplanted from her yard are in a memorial garden at the museum. Also in the garden is the weather station Lil manned every day for twenty-five years. She was a member of the Ground Observer Corps.

Politics did not escape Lil's notice. In 1952 she worked on the campaign that saw Ralph Chetwynd elected to BC's first Social Credit government under Premier W.A.C. Bennett. Critics joked that Premier Bennett's main supporters were "little old ladies in running shoes," but if the others were anything like Lil, it's no wonder his government was elected seven times in a row. During the years the Cariboo was represented by a Social Credit MLA, Lil went to bat for people regardless of their political stripe. Along with stoutly supporting the Social Credit party, she served as deputy returning officer and poll clerk in provincial elections.

Lil had very strong opinions on almost everything and didn't hesitate to share them. For some years the local radio station had an open mic program and she was a regular contributor, often first on the line. Station manager Bob Leckie, who hosted the program, was a true gentleman but she sometimes tried his patience.

Over the years the PGE subdivision disappeared, leaving only the Deschene home and the Station House, which is now an art gallery. As the city moved "up-town" her neighbours were hikers and mountain bikers on the trails on the river valley side of the property, and street people on the town side. Ed died in 1977, shortly after he retired, but Lil refused to move.

Over the years Lil was plagued with ill health, and when the children were young she spent time in the hospital while her mother looked after them. Later she suffered from allergies and arthritis, but that didn't stop her from walking four long blocks to the supermarket or around town on other business. In 2001 she had cancer surgery, and while that slowed her down, she was always in good spirits.

What goes around comes around. When Lil's health eventually failed, friends and people she had helped along the way were there to return the favour. She was as gracious receiving help as she always was giving it. In her last months, her children came home to care for her and she died peacefully in the little green house.

The property belonged to BC Railway, and the lease ended with Lil's death. The house was not in good shape, and the railway didn't want responsibility for it, so the family had it demolished. It was believed to be the oldest family home left in Williams Lake. The lilacs remained. It's a pretty spot on the banks of the Williams Lake River Valley. Many hoped the property would become a park, but that didn't happen.

Gwen Ringwood

She Changed the Character of Williams Lake

Gwen Pharis Ringwood, an outstanding pioneer in western drama and theatre, was well established as a playwright when she came to Williams Lake in 1953 with her doctor husband, Barney Ringwood. Williams Lake was a smallish town then, and Dr. Ringwood, a surgeon, came to join his friend Hugh Atwood, the area's lone doctor.

The Ringwoods fell in love with the Cariboo. Gwen found inspiration in what she called the beautiful mosaic—a colourful cross-section of humanity in harmony with the land. The Ringwoods lived in town until Barney retired in 1968 and they moved to their lakeshore summer home on acreage at Chimney Lake. Both Gwen and Barney enjoyed riding; they had horses and were members of the local Trail Riders.

Gwen shared her considerable talents with the community. She revitalized the local Player's Club by writing and directing plays for members (she was given the club's first lifetime membership in 1968). She held drama classes and writing classes for all ages and encouraged the whole community to get involved one way or an-other. She wrote skits and sketches for coffee house entertainments and service club

Playwright Gwen Ringwood, pictured here at her home in Chimney Lake, brought the theatre to Williams Lake.

fundraisers, and adjudicated both adult and student plays. She worked with students at St. Joseph's Mission and wrote children's plays relating to the mission. In 1967 she joined forces with local musician and composer Art Rosoman to write and direct *The Road Runs North,* a musical celebrating Canada's centennial. The play had a cast of sixty and was a huge success. She did all this while continuing to write and contribute to the drama scene at the provincial and national levels.

Gwen was born in Anatone, Washington, on August 13, 1910. She spent her first years in small communities in southern Alberta where her parents taught school and farmed. Gwen grew up close to the land. In 1926 the family moved to a farm in Montana and Gwen attended university there. When the farm failed, the family moved back to McGrath, Alberta. Gwen worked as a bookkeeper for a time before continuing her studies at the University of Alberta. She graduated with honours in 1934 with a bachelor of arts degree.

Her interest in drama began as a youngster when she attended performances by travelling theatre groups. In high school she acted in plays, and during her time at university, Gwen worked for the Department of Extension's director of drama. She was later registrar at the Banff Centre for the Arts, and while she was there she began writing radio plays. In 1935 she wrote her first play, *The Dragons on Kent.* In 1937 she won a Rockefeller Foundation fellowship that allowed her to go to the University of North Carolina where she earned her master's degree in dramatic writing. She wrote five plays in the two years she was there. One of them, *Still Stands the House,* a spooky, one-act play, became one of the most frequently performed plays in the history of Canadian theatre. In 1939 it won first prize at the Dominion Drama Festival.

In 1940, Gwen returned to the University of Alberta as director of dramatics. That same year she married Dr. John Brian (Barney) Ringwood. The couple spent two years in northern Saskatchewan where Barney practised medicine before joining the Army Medical Corps. He was in the service for four years. While living in Edmonton during the war, Gwen received a grant from Robert Gard of the Alberta Folklore and Local History Project to write Alberta folk plays. *Jack the Joker* told the story of the colourful Calgary newspaper editor, Bob Edwards; *The Rainmaker* was set in Medicine Hat during the drought of 1921; and *Stampede* was about a black cowboy and rancher. She also wrote *Widgers Way,* which became a favourite with amateur groups. She began writing for radio and co-authored a series of history plays featuring great names in history, such as Socrates, Beethoven and Florence Nightingale. She focused on their social and personal lives as well as their achievements. In 1941 she received the Governor General's Medal for outstanding service in the development of Canadian drama.

After the war the Ringwoods lived in Lamont, Alberta, and Edmonton before coming to Williams Lake with their four children, Stephen, Susan, Carol and Patrick.

Gwen was much in demand in BC as a lecturer, teacher and adjudicator. She worked with both the Central Interior Arts Panel and the BC Arts Board. In 1973 she won the Eric Hamber trophy, and in 1975 her work in amateur theatre was recognized when she was named honourary president of the BC Drama Association. In 1981 she received a doctorate in fine arts from the University of Victoria, and a year later an honourary Doctor of Laws from the University of Lethbridge.

Gwen's early work reflected life on the prairies, and her later work, life in the Cariboo. In her later years she was concerned about social injustices and this too was reflected in her work. In 1982 *The Collective Plays of Gwen Pharis Ringwood*, a 590-page anthology of her plays was published. She was the first Canadian playwright to be anthologized. That same year, the University of Calgary purchased her memorabilia including all the plays (including radio plays), stories, books, poems and musicals she had written since 1935. As Gwen was a prolific writer and won many awards, this is a big collection. She also was much written about, including a biocritical essay written by Dr. Geraldine Anthony.

Gwen died in 1984 at her Chimney Lake home. She was seventy-three. To quote the late *Tribune* publisher Clive Stangoe, who knew Gwen well, "Her impact on Williams Lake changed the character of the place."

Mary Ann Ross

Some Cowboys Were Women

The Cariboo Chilcotin cattle country is well known for its legendary cowboys. Some of those cowboys were women like Mary Ann Ross, who could outride, outrope and outshoot the best of them. She was equally talented in the "women's work" department, being top-notch in both cooking and handiwork.

Mary Ann's father was George Turner, an American who came to the Chilcotin country around 1900. Her mother, Louisa, was the daughter of Tsilhqot'in Chief One Eye. A lake near the Chilcotin community of Kleena Kleene is named for him. Mary Ann was born at Kleena Kleene in 1918.

There was some mystery about George Turner. Some said he was on the run from US lawmen but there was reason to believe it was US outlaws he was avoiding. Whatever the story, he always packed a brace of pistols and was cautious of strangers.

George ran cattle on his ranch and trapped in the Chilcotin, Knights Inlet and Bella Coola areas. Mary Ann learned about trapping, hunting, and the outdoors from him. She learned the traditional Tsilhqot'in ways, including the language and survival skills, from Louisa, and horsemanship from both of them. Louisa was still breaking wild horses when she was in her late sixties, in spite of having a crippled arm. Mary Ann was a daring rider like her mother. Old-timers told stories of how she chased wild horses through the bush while riding bareback.

Although their home was in the remote west Chilcotin, the Turners lived well. The daughters always had the latest clothes from Eaton's catalog. Mary Ann was good-looking and had a great sense of style. Her working clothes were the usual shirts, jeans, boots and a wide-brimmed cowboy hat. When she was younger she wore a shell-studded gun belt (sometimes holding a six-shooter) and a bolo tie or a bright scarf. When the occasion called for more formal wear she dressed accordingly and it was hard to picture this handsome lady in the stylish dress herding cows or shooting moose.

Mary Ann could tell some stories. One was about a neighbour's Black Angus bull. The neighbour bought the bull to enhance his herd, but he couldn't, or wouldn't, keep it fenced in. It kept getting in with everyone's cows and nobody appreciated this breeding program. Mary Ann and her sister, teenagers at the time, were tired of chasing the bull away from their herd. When it made the mistake of paying a visit one day when the girls were alone on the ranch, they managed to get him into their corral and then rope and castrate him.

Mary Ann Ross was tiny, but she liked to ride a big horse. She learned about ranching and hunting from her American father, and the traditional skills from her Tsilhqot'in mother.

When telling this story years later, Mary Ann said the bull's owner was furious but he never found out who did it. "Nobody blamed us, nobody thought we could do it," she would say with a chuckle.

Mary Ann married Jim Ross, who ranched at Redstone with his brothers. Jim's father, Ralph Ross, came from Nova Scotia around the turn of the century, established the ranch, and married Susan Charlieboy. Jim sold his share of the ranch and he and Mary Ann bought a place at Charlotte Lake, many miles from anywhere. All was well until grizzly bears began hanging around the place and Mary Ann feared for the children's safety. The oldest were school age by that time, so they sold the ranch and moved to the Knoll Ranch at Chezacut where there was a school and no grizzlies.

After Chezacut, Jim and Mary Ann worked at the 150 Mile Ranch for twelve years, then moved about a bit until returning to the Chilcotin to work at the C1 Ranch for Dieter and Ilse Kellinghusen. They were there for thirty years before retiring to Williams Lake.

The Rosses had twelve children, and Mary Ann was an excellent cook and a caring mom. The children were always well fed, well dressed and well mannered.

When the children were older, she worked outside with Jim. They came as a

For many years Mary Ann and her husband Jim worked at the CI ranch at Alexis Creek where Mary Ann was considered to be the top cowboy.

set. Everything Mary Ann did, she did well, be it putting up hay, feeding, branding, rounding up cattle or riding the range. She was the top rider at the C1. She rode with the cattle in remote ranges until she was well into her seventies. She'd stay with the herd all summer, watching that they didn't overgraze and keeping an eye out for predators, injuries or disease.

Mary Ann was tiny, but she liked to ride a big horse, one that could carry her all day. She never seemed to tire and would spend the entire day in the saddle, never resting until the cattle were all where they were supposed to be. She always had a dog to help herd the cattle, ward off bears and keep her company. She rode slowly, slapping her quirt on her batwing chaps, quietly moving the cattle along and keeping them in line. (By the time she retired, the chaps were all but worn out.) She had no patience with "whoop and holler" cowhands, and she let them know about it. She had a good sense of humour but even the toughest cowboys learned not to cross her.

The weather didn't bother her, although she did get fed up when it rained at haying time. "Too bad nobody can turn that off," she'd say. She wore a bright yellow slicker, rubber gloves and boots when it rained.

Mary Ann was a great hunter, and she was still hunting when she was in her eighties, her eyesight and aim as good as ever. No one remembers her coming home empty-handed. Jim said when they were out in the bush she always carried the gun. She would not only shoot moose and deer, she'd butcher them, tan their hides, and make jackets, gloves and moccasins. She did original handwork in the Tsilhqot'in tradition and it annoyed her when younger people working in buckskin strayed from the traditional designs in beadwork or embroidery.

Mary Ann had her share of sorrows. She lost three sons. Jim was ill after they retired, and she cared for him until he died. She came to the end of her trail in 2001 and passed away in Deni House, the seniors' residential care facility in Williams Lake.

2

WOMEN OF DISTINCTION

Marta Deak

From Hungary to the Cariboo

By Marta Deak

I was born in the Transylvanian community of Zilah, now Zilau, in June 1928. The area had been a part of Hungary since 896 AD, but was given to Romania together with some three million ethnic Hungarians by the Treaty of Versailles in 1919, after the First World War.

My parents, John and Ida Keresztes, were a loving and caring couple. My father, a railway clerk, was pushed around the country by his Romanian superiors from one location to another simply because he was Hungarian, always working in the shadow of prejudice and ethnic hatred. He was a tall, handsome man, kind, well-liked and respected in his circle. He spoke sixteen languages fluently.

Mother never unpacked our things; she always had to be ready to move and ready for new challenges. She was a beautiful and resourceful lady who could create something from virtually nothing to keep us fed and clothed. I can remember many things, as I was always carefully observing, asking questions, tucking everything away into my memory. I was the only child and Mother was my constant companion. We could never stay long enough at any place to have friends. Even as a child I could feel the everyday pressures my parents coped with, trying to make ends meet during the Great Depression.

I started school in 1935, when I was seven, and continued in a Hungarian language school for two years. Then Dad was transferred into the heart of Romania and I had to learn my first new language from scratch. There was no such thing as special coaching. By the end of the term I spoke the Romanian language and passed my third grade.

The hate and bullying I experienced from the other kids, and even the teachers, is unforgettable and unforgivable. Dad told me I had to be strong and stand up for my rights. It was the worst school year of my life. The following years were always interrupted, as we had to keep moving to new areas. Dad never knew where he'd be stationed next. He had to follow the orders or lose his job.

Mom and I travelled long distances by train to see Dad. It was a great opportunity to see the country. We lived in large cities and small villages, from Bucharest, Romania's capital city, to Constance, a busy seaport. In 1940 we lived for a short time in Turnu Severin, located on the Danube bordering Yugoslavia. In August that year a summit held among the major European powers agreed to the temporary return of parts of Transylvania to Hungary. Dad decided we should move back to Hungary. We crossed the border a month later.

For me it was a new beginning, new surroundings and a new school, where I had to relearn the Hungarian language. This time I managed to stay for four years in the same junior high school in the city of Nagyvarad, now once again called Oradea and back in Romania.

When Hungary joined Germany in attacking the Soviet Union in the summer of 1941, things got very bad, very fast. Shortages of food, clothing, and the rationing of everything led to the growth of the black market. Mother and I made trips to nearby villages to buy the necessities to supplement our food rations. We had to travel by train at night to avoid being arrested as it was illegal to buy, or even to possess, extra food.

The first American bombardment of the city happened on June 6, 1944. Our home was close to the large railway station, an important target. We got used to the air raids, but our nerves were always on edge. I'll never forget the clear summer day when we were out in the back yard and the sirens went on. We looked up and spotted the lead plane in the first block of planes releasing something shiny. We barely made it to the cellar when the bombs started to fall. The air pressure from the explosions was unbearable. I thought my ears would burst. It only lasted a minute or two. The bombers missed the railway station and switching yards, but the damage and casualties in the residential areas were terrible, as was the case all over Europe. Two months later the railway and widespread residential areas were wiped out by American bombers using carpet bombing, which was when all the planes released their bombs simultaneously, causing terrible damage. Our home was destroyed, but luckily we'd left the city a short time before.

All large buildings were converted into hospital facilities caring for wounded soldiers and civilians. Hungary was under German occupation from March 1944, when the Germans discovered the government, under Admiral Nicholas Horthy, was negotiating to have the Western Allies occupy the country to prevent a Soviet occupation.

The food shortage was getting worse as the Russians were getting closer. The war was just next door, with heavy artillery going on all night, lighting up the sky. The roads were jammed with military convoys. Dad was out every night trying to find out what the situation really was. Then early one morning he came in and told us we had to leave.

Mom was calm. She spread a sheet on the floor and started tossing whatever she thought were valuable items onto it, including clothing and bedding. I still have some of the photographs, documents, and beautiful handwork she saved in those terrible moments of our life, in October 1944. We have always treasured the contents of what was known as the Magic Sheet in our family.

We left Transylvania forever, getting a ride in a German military truck, then continued to Western Hungary, living in the small village of Alsoszolnok, close to the Austrian border. A kind old couple gave us a room and shelter for the next five months, letting us cook in their small kitchen. Dad was on duty every other day at the railway station at the border town of Szent Gotthard, documenting and releasing trains across the border. He was commuting by horse and cart until he fell at his workplace during the blackout, injuring his knee, which put him on sick leave.

The situation was bad by the spring of 1945. The Russians were coming closer. Nobody knew what the next day was going to bring. We packed our meager belongings and left Hungary with the horse and cart on March 29, 1945, never to return. Money was worthless, but Dad bought lots of tobacco before we left, the only valuable currency for trading on the black market, so we could survive on whatever we could get and feed our horse.

It was a long and arduous journey, walking across Austria, mostly at night to avoid air raids. The roads were strafed by the American fighters during the days. It took us four weeks of wandering, crossing several high passes in the Alps, starving, facing storms and real cold. Dad couldn't walk with his injured leg and had to sit on the wagon. Mother and I attended to everything. Our clothing was poor, and I only had city shoes. We walked, leading the horse by the head as she was scared of all the turmoil on the night roads packed with thousands of refugees. We were hoping our journey would end somewhere, one day. A few times we were lucky and could rest at night in barns with cows keeping us warm, getting milk from the odd kindly farmer. I was sixteen and those days are the only grey areas in my memory. I don't know how we survived all the terrible events and situations we had to face.

We were told to proceed toward Germany for safety, but that was a big lie. When we arrived at Passau on the River Danube, the military border guard promptly told us to go back to where we came from. It took us two weeks to reach that German border and by then we knew that the war was lost for our side. The night roads were jammed with military trucks, equipment, horse wagons, refugees and prisoners of war, starving and in ragged uniforms. Everybody was trying to survive and solve their own problems. We hoped to get back to Hungary, but that never happened.

May 5, 1945, I remember as a miserable, wet day, staying with some other refugees in a small guest house. Suddenly, the area was filled with loud shouting, yelling and singing: "The war has ended!" We couldn't believe our ears. This was on the West side. On the East side the war ended three days later, on May 8. We had the momentary hope everything would be fine. It didn't last. The borders were closed in a very short time and we started hearing of Russian atrocities, the gang raping of women, the gathering and taking away of thousands into prison camps, the gulags.

After days of wandering over the most vicious back-road mountain passes, we ended up in the small community of Obertraun surrounded by high mountains, on the Hallstatter Lake. The only road leading out of that valley was closed and we were stuck.

There was a makeshift, primitive military hospital in a former artillery training camp full of wounded, mostly amputees. The whole mountain area of Austria was full of hospitals; every hotel, school and guest house was jammed with the wounded, whose wounds couldn't heal because of the starvation rations they received. Mom and Dad got jobs in the hospital washing clothes and everything by hand, and looking after the boilers. I cleaned the huts, around the patients, with just plain water and a mop, no rubber gloves or soap or disinfectants, yet there were no infections. We all had well-working immune systems then. It was hard work, but we received some food, a room in a hut and minimum wage, but the money couldn't buy anything.

I met Ed, who was recovering from a leg wound caused by a mortar shell, later in the fall, on a Sunday afternoon walk with my parents. We heard somebody whistling a Hungarian tune. Dad said it must be a Hungarian as nobody else could whistle a tune like that. We'd seen each other before in the hospital yard, but that was our formal introduction, an important thing in our society at the time.

When the hospital closed we moved to a nice place, rented from a local family. We kept the connection with them for many years after. When a small hand-weaving business opened up in one of the former prisoner-of-war huts, Dad and I got jobs making rugs from strips cut from old clothing. Later we received looms and steady jobs. Ed was working for the US Army in the city of Wels when he came down with an infected appendicitis. After he recovered, he got a job in our shop as a hand weaver, making clothing and upholstery materials. By the time we left in 1948 the shop had about a dozen employees.

We couldn't, and really didn't want to, stay in Austria, or even in Europe any longer. We were looking for an opportunity to emigrate and find homes somewhere in the world away from the constant wars, shortages and starvation, the typical repetitions of European history. But the world was choosy about whom to pick from the millions of refugees. The applicants' ages and national background were always up front. For Mom and Dad it was almost impossible to start a new life somewhere at their age. Ed and I were madly in love, without any hope for any future together, but we waited for a miracle.

Marta and Ed Deak met in Hungary toward the end of WWII, and were reunited in England after the war was over.

And the miracle happened. In 1948, at the beginning of the Cold War, the British government needed young people, especially with military experience, to work as a kind of reserve, in case of an open war with the Soviets. We both volunteered, and passed all the medical and political examinations. Our plan was that I'd go first and then try to get my parents out, but it didn't work out that way.

Ed left a week ahead of me. My poor parents were very upset, losing their only child, but I had to go as there was no future for any of us in Austria, where people hated us and most of them called us "damned foreigners." The pain of parting from Ed haunted me all the way, and I feared that I may never see him again. But there was no other way, only the hope in our hearts that things would work out and one day we'd be together.

Our miracle worked once again. After a long wait for transport in a camp at Asten, Austria, I left by British military train for Munster, in West Germany, with hundreds of other young people to a camp in a former German barracks complex. There we went through the same health and political examinations. Then I met up with Ed, just before his transport left for England. It was a very happy, joyous

Marta had to learn to speak English in a hurry when she was given a job in a hospital in England. With a good place to live and good food to eat, she thought she was in heaven after the brutal days spent in war-torn Europe.

moment to find each other once again. Three years after the war many people in Munster were still living in holes underground, in the basements of bombed-out buildings. Where there were once many comfortable homes standing, now were all ruins everywhere.

The last leg of the trip came by train across Holland, then by ship from the Hook of Holland near Rotterdam, across the English Channel to Harwich, and we were in England, which we had heard so much about. Our reception was warm and kind. We were handed two ten shilling notes, or a pound, of spending money, as a gift from King George. We had no idea where we were going when we boarded trains for a long journey to a camp in Liverpool on the west coast. We stayed there for some time, and we had decent beds and food to eat before we were selected to various work places. I ended up in a seniors' home/hospital at Dutton, near Warrington, with a friend, Herci, I met on our trip from Austria.

I was twenty years old when I started my new life. I didn't speak a word of English, had no experience in anything whatsoever, and no idea about what to expect, or what was expected of me. At the hospital we were greeted with the greatest kindness. We were fitted with new nurses' uniforms and then ushered to beautiful, private living quarters, for the first time in our lives. I'll never forget that feeling, with plenty of food I hadn't seen for years, pleasant surroundings. The staff were nice, we were working side by side with them, attending to the patients, carefully watching every move while listening to the flow and sound of the new language. In six months I'd learned enough to carry on a conversation.

Ed came to visit me for a couple of days. We hadn't seen each other for a long time, but we hoped things would work out for us. He was working on a farm at Hardwick, near Cambridge, but distance kept us apart. In the spring of

1949 I decided to get a transfer to a hospital at Cambridge. It was a hassle but I ended up in a maternity hospital as a domestic helper. I stayed there for two years.

Hardwick was only about eight kilometres from Cambridge. I had a new three-speed Raleigh bicycle, Ed had a motorcycle he used to go to classes in town, so we could see each other every few days and plan for our future, while improving our language and skills by taking evening courses in various subjects.

We wanted to marry, but the housing situation was atrocious, with people living in all kinds of holes and calling them home. Finally, we had an offer for a place on the farm, owned by Chivers Jams, where Ed was working, and our dream of being together came through, after six years. We married on March 30, 1951. It was a simple occasion, but one of the happiest days of our lives. We

Marta and Ed arrived in Canada in 1955. After spending some time in Montreal they climbed onto their Douglas motorcycle and travelled to Vancouver. Marta says it was a magical journey.

saved our money, bought our beloved Douglas motorcycle, and travelled all over England. We used the bike later to cross Canada. That bike was the best wedding present to ourselves and is now on exhibit in the Williams Lake Museum.

Our stay in England was pleasant; we had friends we could get together with on weekends, visiting historical places, castles, and the usual English seaside areas. But our hearts were telling us we had to look for a new home where we could settle down and have a family.

My parents were sponsored by a church group to emigrate to the USA and were living in Portland, Oregon. They made arrangements for us to move there, and we had our papers ready, but then one of Ed's friends, who moved to America six months before, was called into the US Army. We had to sign a paper agreeing Ed would be ready for the draft four days after our arrival. That was a serious matter for us. With the Korean war going full blast there was a chance for Ed ending up in another war, barely escaping with his life in the previous one. That was too much even to think about. We stayed in England and waited for the opportunity to come to Canada. Later, every time we went down to the States for any reason, we could hardly wait to get back home to Canada.

We came to Canada in April 1955 as British citizens. We stayed in Montreal for a few days then got onto our Douglas and started across the country. The experience was almost magical all the way. There was hope and beauty in the air, right across this huge country everywhere we went. We passed abandoned homesteads across the prairies, where once hard-working families lived, but all that was left were their memories. Old machinery rusting in the yards, lace curtains blowing through broken windows. But life goes on and the memory of our unforgettable four weeks on the road will be cherished and stay with us forever. That was before the Trans-Canada Highway was completed and in many places we were on back roads of sand, hundreds of miles on gravel and many times on mud, where we could hardly keep the bike upright and I had to walk behind. We met kind people who offered us jobs and housing. The temptation was great, but we were set for Vancouver to be close to my parents in Portland.

Vancouver was a pleasant place then. The traffic was minimal and, to the best of my recollection, the Hotel Vancouver was perhaps the tallest building. Our stay in the city lasted twenty-four years. We raised our two girls and a boy, while learning skills, trades and collecting experiences all the time. Ed, who was a trained artist by then, learned to make high quality custom furniture and opened his own shop in 1957. We built our own energy-efficient, ultra-modern home. But by the early seventies, we could feel growing pressures. The city was getting too big. The traffic was worse by the day, everything became more expensive. Working ten- to- twelve-hour

Marta and Ed have made their home in the Cariboo since 1979. Ed says he has gotten old, but in his eyes, Marta is still seventeen.

days in the business, seven days a week, was getting us down.

Dad passed away in 1973. We brought Mom to Burnaby where we could visit her all the time. She passed away in 1975. We missed them a lot.

I inherited some money from them and had to decide what to do with it. Ed didn't want any part in the decision making. For a long time I had the idea of getting out of the city. We built a cabin at Hawkins Lake in 1970 and were spending our holidays there. The lot was close to an acre and for us it was huge, compared to our thirty-three-foot lot in the city. The charm of the Cariboo got to us and we went for long rides, looking around and thinking how nice it would be to have a larger piece of land where we could live in peace and quiet.

One day we drove by Big Lake looking for land that was listed for sale, off the main road. The road was so bad we had to park our van and walk in. The place was a terrible mess of garbage and broken glass, with rats and mice running all around, run-down shacks, an old log barn filled with three feet of manure, and an old log house, filled with garbage and rodent droppings. But I had a vision that we could do something with the place.

That was on the Thanksgiving weekend in 1975. I couldn't get Big Lake out of my mind. I told Ed in November that I would like to go back and take another look, with the intention of buying it.

We made arrangements with a real estate office in Williams Lake to look at the place. I was working as a gift wrapper at the Woodward's store in Vancouver at the time. Ed picked me up at the store, and we hit the road. We stopped at a Clinton motel for a few hours' sleep, then took off again just as the first snow of the winter started coming down.

We left Williams Lake with the agent in a blizzard that continued all day. We walked around the perimeter of the land and decided right then where we'd build our home. When we got back to our snowed-up van, I made an offer. It was accepted the next day. It took us four years to settle our affairs and sell everything in Vancouver. Meanwhile we cleaned up the old log house for storage, built a couple of cabins where we could stay when we came up for visits, and made preparations for our move.

When we moved up in the spring of 1979, we set up the log house as a workshop and started building a large, three-level house where we could live and work comfortably on our art and other indoor projects. We had no electricity, no phone, no refrigeration, no running water, but we were free and happy on our own land. We were complete greenhorns who had to learn how to survive all alone in the forest, how to grow things, raise animals and birds, milk a cow, things we'd never done before, to become self-sufficient to the highest degree. We started our pioneering under the most simple and almost primitive conditions.

I wanted to learn everything, how to make butter and cheese, raise chickens,

pigs and rabbits, how to butcher and grow things organically on a land with practically no topsoil, five-month winters, frost in just about every summer month and
winter temperatures down to forty-five below for weeks. The word "organic" was
almost unknown and lots of people made fun of me but we had enough of chemical
agriculture in England and we never wanted to see any chemicals on our land. We
succeeded very well and after a few years we had a fairly large commercial garden
where we were growing vegetables strictly organically and without any bugs. We're
still raising organic calves.

We started building our home right away, but we hardly got the first floor
framed when we found out we wouldn't get paid for the Vancouver business. Here
we were sitting in the wilderness virtually penniless, but at least without any debts.
We built another small cabin as our working room for sewing and artwork and
started looking to see if we could make a living building custom furniture with a
small generator and doing whatever odd jobs we could find. Ed had good connec-
tions with some art galleries in Vancouver but they went broke in 1980 and we lost
our major income possibility. We never gave up and survived all the odds. We only
had our son, John, living with us at the time. He served his apprenticeship with Ed
as a custom furniture maker after he graduated from high school, and then left and
went in other directions.

It took us eight and a half years to get the phone and electricity and finish the
house to where we could finally move in on Christmas Day 1987. We never had a
better Christmas present before or after.

When I look back, I have to wonder how life is cut out for anybody and which
way it leads us. The misery of the war and its aftermath, the starvation and hardships
of the refugee years brought Ed and I together. We'd never have met under normal
circumstances. Our life was shaped step by step to lead us in a certain direction, but
every minute of it was worth it for us. We had to learn languages, crafts, trades, and
had to come halfway around the world to find our real home, but we made it and
made the best of every minute of our fortune of being together. The Cariboo was
calling us in all those years. We came running to answer its call and we never again
could leave.

Author's note:
What with one thing and another, Marta Deak didn't start painting seriously until
she was in her seventies and realized she could express the beauty she felt within
her. She began making greeting cards for friends and family, then with the help and
advice of her husband, Ed, an accomplished artist, she began painting seriously.
Watercolours are her forte, as she says she was intimidated by oils. Marta's studio is
on the top floor of the Deak home in the peaceful Big Lake Valley. It is a long way
from Transylvania, Hungary, where she was born.

Donna Barnett

The Cariboo's First Female MLA

Donna Barnett is known in the Cariboo as a hard-working politician who gets things done. However, the fact that she was the first woman mayor of the District of 100 Mile House and the first woman elected to represent the Cariboo Chilcotin in the BC legislature mostly goes unremarked.

Donna's political career began in 1974 when she volunteered to campaign for Alex Fraser, the long-time, well-respected Cariboo MLA. She was active with the Social Credit Party until its demise, then joined the BC Liberal Party. She had an impressive track record for community involvement long before she was elected mayor in 1986, and during her years in municipal politics she served on a wide variety of committees, boards and agencies. When she was elected as South Cariboo MLA (now Cariboo Chilcotin) she brought a diverse background to the job.

Donna Nelson was born in Vancouver in 1942. She was raised on a small farm in Richmond (near Steveston) with two older brothers. She attended Lord Byng Elementary until the family moved to Burnaby in 1956, and she completed her education there. As a teenager her main interests were sports, music and dancing, not necessarily in that order. She met Jack Barnett at junior high school. He was actually going with her girlfriend at the time, but in 1960 she and Jack were married. Before their marriage they bought property in Port Moody for twelve hundred dollars with no down payment and payments of forty dollars a month.

Donna worked for the *Vancouver Province*, then Simpsons-Sears. In the early 1960s, Jack was working as a sheet metal journeyman mechanic for a local company. The owner's brother owned the Exeter Arms Hotel in 100 Mile House, and in 1964 Jack went with his boss to do some work at the hotel. He was intrigued by the South Cariboo country. He took the family back to spend weekends in the area, where they enjoyed the outdoors, especially snowmobiling in winter.

"We improved the land the hard way."

The Barnetts had used their equity in the Port Moody property as a down payment for a new house in Coquitlam. In 1966 they sold that home and moved to a larger place in Burnaby so they could look after Jack's father. However, the Cariboo was very much on their minds. "It was Jack's passion to move to the Cariboo, so we did," Donna says.

In 1965, they had bought 240 acres at 96 Mile House. They paid $4,500 for bare rocky land that had no road access. It's one and a half kilometres from where a subdivision is now—Barnett Road is named for them. "We improved the land the hard way," Donna says. "We worked with hand tools, and with the help of Ian Gilpin, we built a road, drilled a well, and put in a septic tank."

They put a 46-by-8-foot trailer onto the property and with their two sons, aged three and eight months old, they moved to the Cariboo to stay in the spring of 1967. The trailer was quite a switch from their 1,400-square foot, full-basement, completely finished home, and 100 Mile House was a far cry from Burnaby, but the Barnetts embraced the country life. They had a quarter horse with a colt, and Jack had Welsh ponies and raced in the chuckwagon/chariot circuit. Donna worked at the Exeter Arms Hotel for their first two years in the Cariboo.

They were founding members of the 100 Mile Snowmobile Club, and Donna served as secretary, then president of the group. Later they were involved with the development of an extensive snowmobile trail system. Their interest in the sport led them to use the homestead as a down payment to buy the 93 Mile Sales and Service, a Ski-Doo dealership. "Neither of us had a clue about running a business," Donna recalls.

In wintertime the South Cariboo's snowy backcountry and frozen lakes make it ideal for snowmobiling, and as the 100 Mile community grew, so did interest in the sport. The Barnetts built a new facility and changed the business name to "100 Mile Recreational Sales and Service," which opened officially in 1971. When they sold the business, Donna went into real estate and worked as a licensed realtor until 2006.

Over the years Donna has been involved in many organizations, and the line between her official and volunteer work is blurred. Along with her boundless energy, she has good organizational skills, and she was much in demand by community groups. She worked with numerous organizations including the Outriders Club and ladies softball and she helped raise money to build the Stan Halcro Arena. She's been involved with the 100 Mile House Museum Society, the Lower Bridge Creek Watershed Society, the South Cariboo Chamber of Commerce and the 1986 legacy project (which saw the building of the visitor info centre in 100 Mile House). She is a Rotarian, Kiwanian and a charter member of the 100 Mile Kinettes.

Donna's philosophy is "if something needs doing, then do it" and it was a logical step from leading community groups to running for mayor in 1986. She took a break in 1990, but was elected to the mayor's chair again six years later. As mayor, she was involved in a wide range of municipal affairs, including the 100 Mile and District Safety Committee, the Spirit of BC 100 Mile House Community Committee, and Measuring Up the North.

She co-chaired the Council of Resource Community Mayors, chaired the South Cariboo Planning Council, and was part of the federal Natural Resources Committee and the premier's Climate Action Team. She has been with the Cariboo Regional District and Hospital District and the Millsite and Fisher Place South Cariboo Health facilities, along with seniors' low-cost housing, which were built while she was mayor.

Her experiences included Community Policing, the Premier's Task Force on Opportunities, Land Use Planning, Restorative Justice Committee, and Regional Economic Development. She had a hand in education with BC Open Learning Agency and was a director on the Cariboo College board when the Williams Lake campus was opened. Her council was responsible for boundary expansions and numerous infrastructure projects. She worked with the 100 Mile Soccer Association in building the soccer fields. Under her watch, the fire department training centre was built, and the woodlot and community forest developed. Her council worked with Ainsworth Company in 1990 to build the OSB plant, believed to be the first in North America. She was with the Regional Economic Development group that did the feasibility study for the generation plant in Williams Lake to clean up air quality there.

By the early 2000s, the mountain pine beetle (MPB) attack on Cariboo Chilcotin forests was out of control. While the beetle-attacked trees provided a short-term bonanza for local mills, it was clear there would be problems when they were gone. Donna was a founding member of the Cariboo Chilcotin Beetle Action Coalition, which saw municipal and First Nations leaders work with communities, industry and conservation groups to find ways to diversify the local economy.

The Industrial Hemp Production Pilot Project is an example of how Donna matched words with action. In 2003 when resident Jack Witty approached her and suggested growing industrial hemp as an economic possibility, Donna got the wheels going. They established a ten-person board, including representatives from the Canim Lake First Nations, and went to work. It took six years of struggle, taking what Donna calls "little steps," before the federal government came up with funding to launch a pilot project. The government found industrial hemp production would indeed be a viable industry, and the group is currently seeking investors. Donna stepped down from the committee when she was elected MLA but she does whatever she can to promote the project.

Her most traumatic experience as mayor was being notified that the long-serving volunteer fire chief, Bob Paterson, had died from injuries after going to rescue someone in distress. Another time the phone rang telling her the fire hall was on fire. She was the emergency co-ordinator during the terrible fires in Barriere in 2003. That position involved helping 1,400 displaced people.

Donna says her greatest feeling of accomplishment as mayor was planning for the future of the 100 Mile area "and seeing where it has come from to become the well-planned community it is today."

She ran for the position of MLA in 2009 on the Liberal ticket. It was her second try at provincial politics, as she ran unsuccessfully on the Social Credit ticket in 1991. The 2009 election was a cliffhanger. NDP incumbent Charlie Wyse was declared the winner, but a second look gave Donna the win by eighty-eight votes. Premier Gordon Campbell appointed her parliamentary secretary for Pine Beetle Community Recovery to the Ministry of Community and Rural Development in June 2009. She was also named a member of the select standing committees on Aboriginal Affairs, on Health and the committee on Parliamentary Reform, Ethical Conduct, Standing Orders and Private bills. In September 2011 she was named parliamentary secretary for Rural Communities, Sport and Cultural Development.

By 2012, it was clear that most of the pine-beetle-attacked forests had been logged, and forest companies in the BC interior were running out of trees. In May, Premier Christy Clark appointed Donna to the legislative special committee on Midterm Timber Supply. Donna is the only woman on the committee, which was given four months to examine the situation and make recommendations. That meant she had a busy summer. Donna has received a number of personal awards, including the 125th Canadian Government Medal for Community Achievement, South Cariboo Citizen of the Year, Women of the Year in Resource Communities, and the BC Government Community Achievement Award.

When the legislature isn't sitting (and when she isn't involved with committees), Donna spends time between her two constituency offices, one in 100 Mile and one in Williams Lake, and she's on the road a lot, attending events and meeting with constituents in the wide-spread Cariboo Chilcotin. When she has time in her busy schedule, she relaxes by snowmobiling, gardening and baking. She and Jack are classic-car buffs and they were instrumental in bringing Hot July Nights, a classic car and bike show to 100 Mile House. The gathering has become an annual event, attracting hundreds of people to the area. When the roads are good, Donna drives a 1936 Ford touring sedan that she and Jack restored. Jack has a 1952 Chevrolet coupe.

As MLA, Donna's style is very much like that of Alex Fraser. Her door is open to everyone, she welcomes public input and community ideas, and she enjoys working with volunteers and citizens. "When we work together we can make the quality of all our lives a little easier," she says.

Mary Trott

*M*ary Trott originally thought she'd go into nursing, but her family talked her out of it. Her mother said she was too bossy to be a nurse, so she became a doctor instead.

Mary was born and raised in a community in central Bermuda, near Hamilton. Her father was a master cabinetmaker and made some pieces for the royal family, and her mother was a schoolteacher. When Mary was at school, the teachers she liked and respected most were McGill University graduates, and as she had relatives in Montreal, McGill was a logical choice once she had chosen her career. After first acquiring a bachelor of science from McGill, she graduated with a medical degree in 1969. She was so impressed with a female radiology specialist at Montreal Children's Hospital that she chose radiology as her specialty.

When choosing her post-graduate training, Mary realized she'd been in Canada for eight years and hadn't travelled west of Toronto, so she decided to take her internship at St. Paul's Hospital in downtown Vancouver. The location was handy for street people who usually come late at night, so the ER was lively. During internship Mary was offered a job in obstetrics/gynecology but she still preferred radiology. She says in her first year she did barium enemas all day then went home and did them in her dreams at night.

She was introduced to mammography at this time as well. The machine, she recalls, had a big latex balloon to compress the breast. The X-ray procedure table was high and Mary is short, so she asked for a platform to be built so she could reach her patients. Because she was the only woman resident, she became very good at doing certain X-rays on women with incontinence problems because the male doctors (and the patients) preferred to have a woman do this somewhat delicate procedure.

She did her second-year residency at Vancouver General Hospital (VGH). During that time, she went to the Armed Forces Institute of Pathology at the Pentagon in Washington, DC, for a two-month fellowship, an extensive course in radiologic-pathologic correlation. She also spent time at the BC Health Centre for Children with two very good pediatric radiologists, Dr. Betty Wood and Dr. Donald Newman. During the third year of the residency program, she spent six months in internal medicine and another six months in pathology at Shaughnessy Hospital. Her fourth year was divided between St. Paul's and VGH.

Between internal medicine and pathology, Mary met and married Bernie Littlejohn. The two met at a friend's party in Vancouver. Mary was impressed with neither his haircut nor his opinions on fluoridation. When they met again a few years later, he had a different hairstyle and she didn't recognize him at first, but she did remember his London cockney accent. He remembered her; he'd been looking to renew the acquaintance. At the time Bernie was the maintenance engineer with Canadian Forest Products at the Howe Sound Pulp Mill on the Sunshine Coast, and was in charge of introducing the first successful computerization of the pulp-making process in BC. After their wedding, Mary commuted to the Sunshine Coast on her free weekends. The Friday night ferry waits were usually hours long, and she used that time to continue studying for her fellowship exams.

Bernie wanted to leave the coast, and he was thinking of a small town away from the Lower Mainland. That was fine with Mary; she wanted to work in a small hospital where she would get to know her patients. "I wanted to see them as people, not just images on a screen," she says.

So, in the summer between her third and fourth years, the two spent their holidays travelling around BC looking for a place to settle. Mary applied to a number of hospitals in smaller towns, one of them Williams Lake, which was just the size of community they were looking for. As it happened the incumbent radiologist, Dr. Peter Devito, at Cariboo Memorial Hospital (CMH) also served both Quesnel and 100 Mile House, and he was ready to hand over the growing practice at CMH. Mary did a locum tenens (temporary position) in July 1975 and then worked under his supervision for six months. When she finally became a Fellow of the Royal College of Physicians and Surgeons, he invited her to take over, which she did. "That began my ten-year association with one of BC's best community radiologists," Mary says.

Winter had set in when Mary and Bernie headed for Williams Lake in November 1975. The winter highway was somewhat different than it had been on
their summer jaunts, and they had a hair-raising trip through the canyon. North of
Cache Creek the road was all snow and ice, and it was Mary's introduction to the
many winter trips she was to make up and down Highway 97.

William Speare was the administrator at CMH, and with friends in Victoria he
was good at getting equipment, so at the time the hospital was exceptionally well
equipped for its size. Mary wasn't the first female doctor at CMH but she was the
first full-time woman specialist. On the whole, the medical staff was okay with it;
sometimes they were so busy they didn't know she was there. The hospital at the
time had just over eighty beds. A few of the male physicians had to be handled carefully. Mary says she had to tailor her discussions with one of them so he thought the
decisions were his. She claims radiologists do sometimes get to tell surgeons what
to do.

Staff learned very quickly she wouldn't tolerate any rudeness whatsoever in her
department. "Apologies became voluntary" she remembers, but it was hard to get
the nurses to realize that a radiologist was a real doctor. And then there were the ste-
reotypes. When the medical staff committee held its annual general meeting, Mary
was immediately nominated for secretary. She firmly declined. Later she did take
the job of vice-president on medical staff but she says to get fully involved in the
committee, a doctor needed a wife to take care of things at home and she didn't have
one. However, at her first hospital Christmas party she agreed to play Calpurnia in
the doctors' skit.

Mary and Bernie's first home in Williams Lake was a rented mobile home in a
park overlooking the lake. They knew they were going to stay, so they began looking
for property. They found what they wanted; fifteen acres at Chimney Valley, some
sixteen kilometres and twenty minutes from town. They bought it in 1976 and
moved a mobile home onto it. Bernie wanted to build an underground home, and
it took some research to find plans. The winter Mary was pregnant with daughter
Sonya, the temperature dropped to forty below at the same time the hydro power
went out. All they had for heat was a small wood stove in the mobile home. They
realized that Bernie had better get to work on building a home very soon!

Their 2,400-square-foot house attracted a lot of attention at the time, but it
isn't entirely underground. Three sides snuggle into the hillside, and the front of the
main living area faces onto a south-facing slope. The house is warm in winter and
cool in summer. Bernie had some help with the construction, but he did a lot of
the work himself. It kept him busy for several years. He also managed the business
aspect of Mary's practice.

Mary's pregnancy in 1979 caused some consternation among her colleagues.
She worked until weeks before the birth and then only left when the doctors

persuaded her to go before she had the baby on the job. She planned on taking baby Sonya with her to work for the first few months while she was nursing her, but when the medical staff heard about that they were alarmed, to put it mildly. They sent Dr. Hugh Atwood to give her a fatherly word. He argued that having the baby at work would set a bad example because it would give the nurses ideas and they'd all want to bring their babies to work too.

Mary didn't see the problem. The pace in the hospital back then was leisurely enough that she would have had time to care for Sonya for the first three months, but she gave in to keep the peace. She left Sonya at home and Bernie became "Mr. Mom," which was unusual at the time. "Not taking Sonya to work with me is a decision I've always regretted," Mary says now.

In 1982 CMH was planning to get an ultrasound machine, so Mary spent time at VGH, Lion's Gate and Royal Inland hospitals learning ultrasound. She says it was a good break to be in the company of other radiologists and back in the world of academic medicine again. Another development was mammography. The NDP government made the machines available to community hospitals in BC, and CMH was a logical place for one. Mary made a trip to Vancouver to increase her proficiency in reading the films.

Since retiring, Dr. Mary Trott has more time for community activites. She and husband Bernie Littlejohn enjoy travelling both in Canada and abroad.

For twelve years Mary travelled to 100 Mile House twice a month in all kinds of weather, mostly on her own , although Bernie accompanied her if the road was really bad. Until the Northern Isolation Travel Allowance came in they had no compensation for the trip except the fee for X-ray services rendered, and when the machine broke down, which it sometimes did, she was only paid for the films read while she was there. New developments in radiology have made it possible for local patients to get more specialized examinations without travelling great distances, although some on-the-spot examinations by radiologists are still needed here. In 1990, Dr. Ken MacDonell moved from Kamloops to Williams Lake to share the practice on a fifty-fifty basis, and that gave Mary more time to spend with her family.

One thing unique to the Williams Lake practice was rodeo injuries, which were frequent in the spring and summer. Mary accumulated enough material to write a paper on rodeo radiology, but regrettably never found the time to do it.

Looking back, Mary says practising in a smaller town is very different than practising in the city. In a smaller town the only constant some patients encounter in the health system is the physician they have known all their lives. "One's life is an open book in a small community," Mary notes. "You need a good sense of humour."

She retired in 2002 but she didn't slow down. Grandson Ocean, who is six, lives in Vancouver with Sonya and she sees him as often as she can. She is on the board of the Williams Lake Elder College and occasionally does research and presents courses for the group. She's a counsellor at the seniors' centre, and she belongs to the Quintet Plus singing group. She was involved with the Cariboo Festival during Sonya's school years and since she retired she's become involved again, this time as a performer. She did some locum tenens work in Yellowknife between 1995 and 2004. She's travelled back to Bermuda almost every year to visit family, especially her mother, who is now approaching one hundred years old.

Travel is on her agenda. In 2011 she and Bernie (now eighty-four) enjoyed a Via Rail trip across Canada, and in 2012 they made a trip to England, where Mary says she was treated to some "real" fish and chips.

As for their life in Williams Lake—"When you live in a community for this long, you inevitably put down roots and call it home, wherever you came from initially," Mary says.

Anna Roberts

An Advocate of Conservation

Anna Roberts and her husband, John, came to Williams Lake from Ontario in 1958, newly married. They expected to stay in the Cariboo for a few years before moving on. That few years has stretched to over half a century. John is a veterinarian and a noted local historian. Anna is a naturalist who shares her enthusiasm for and knowledge of nature through her research, teaching, writing, photography and art. She is a strong advocate for conservation and the protection of ecologically important lands. She is also one of the area's foremost potters.

Anna's ancestors were Empire Loyalists who came from the USA during the American Revolution. They settled in southern Quebec. She grew up on the family farm and remembers taking time off school to help gather sap from the maple trees. She was one of four women in a class of 150 at McGill University, graduating in 1951 with a bachelor of science specializing in plant pathology. She went to England hoping to get her master's degree, but when that didn't work out, she spent the summer volunteering at the Rothamsted Research Station working on parasitic plant nematodes. This led to a job back in Canada with the federal government's Science Service in Ottawa. She drove around the countryside collecting and identifying parasitical nematodes. "I've never had the opportunity to look at one since," she says.

Anna met John on a blind date arranged by mutual friends. John, a pilot, came from Melbourne, Australia, in 1950 to attend university and later veterinarian college in Guelph, Ontario. They married after his graduation, came west, and chose the Cariboo when they learned the cattle country needed a veterinarian. Their first home was two wee rooms on Williams Lake's north shore. They often canoed on the lake, and one day some undeveloped acreage on South Lakeside caught their eye. They bought it, and John established the first veterinary clinic north of Kamloops. They had to build a road to the property but being out of the way didn't keep clients from finding them. Anna assisted in the clinic along with raising their three children, Kim, Naomi and Gina.

Anna was fascinated by the incredibly beautiful and virtually untouched Cariboo Chilcotin landscape...

"We came at the right time," Anna says. "There were just enough people to keep us busy without being pushed."

Anna was fascinated by the incredibly beautiful and virtually untouched Cariboo Chilcotin landscape, but she found little recorded information on the area's natural history. Her first step in remedying this was putting together a checklist of local birds. Her interest in birds led to her initiating a Christmas bird count, which started with fifteen participants and is now a major event. For forty-three years she carried out a breeding bird survey each June for the Canadian Wildlife Service. She'd start at dawn, driving along sections of Highway 20, stopping every .8 kilometres to record birds seen or heard singing. After studying and documenting the nesting behaviour of mountain bluebirds, she initiated and, for some years, monitored a nest-box project in the Riske Creek area. The intent was to create a natural biological control of grasshoppers, and according to old-timers in the area, it works.

The incredible number and variety of birds and animals living in the Scout Island marsh caught Anna's attention. The property is close to Williams Lake's downtown area, and she saw it as an ideal spot for an environmental education centre. When the town council bought the island from the Pacific Great Eastern Railway in 1966, she heard opportunity knocking.

The city established a tourist campsite and a public beach on the island, and planned to develop the adjacent marsh until Anna stepped in. She led a delegation of University Women's Club members (all fifteen of them) who persuaded council to study the area before making any decisions. She then helped organize and was the first president of the Williams Lake Field Naturalist Club, which began lobbying to protect the marsh and island. The study recommended the site be developed as a nature centre. After some negotiations, council sold the property to BC Nature Trust, then leased it back. In 1978 the field naturalists took over management of the site as an educational facility for the encouragement and appreciation of nature. The centre features innovative displays, outdoor education programs for adults and children, and a preschool. Anna and her daughters designed many displays. Over the years she has trained staff and developed educational materials and an extensive library. The Island Centre is popular with tourists and residents.

Anna also had a hand in preserving Williams Lake's Boitanio Park. She was a member of the town's recreation commission when the former golf course became a 1971 BC Centennial project. The commission developed a natural park but that didn't last. Boitanio is now a manicured city park, but it has survived numerous threats from development.

Over the years Anna has canoed lakes and rivers and camped in the wilderness to satisfy her curiosity about the natural world of the Cariboo. She's explored local mountains, meadows, old-growth forests, grasslands, wetlands, creek and river valleys, lakes and ponds. Her knowledge has provided the natural history for numerous parks and ecological reserves in the area, including the Williams Lake River Valley and the Doc English Bluff Ecological Reserve. The latter was established after she found a rare plant growing there.

She was working as a consultant for the Cariboo Forest Region when she found native plants that hadn't been identified in this area. She published a field guide to the sedges, and put together a picture key to twenty-two species of native willows. In the early 1990s, Anna and her daughter Gina were working as consultants for the Ministry of Environment when they found a dozen bat species, six previously unknown to this area. The high cliffs above the city of Williams Lake are home to the spotted bat, which wasn't known to occur this far north until the Roberts team found it.

"Nobody knew they were there because no one had looked carefully before," Anna explains. "We really enjoyed studying bats, catching, measuring, and identifying them. Some nights we caught and released at least a hundred of them." They put together a full-page bat article with photos in the *Williams Lake Tribune* in November 1992.

In 1988 Anna co-authored a guide to wetland ecosystems in the dry Douglas fir subzone, and she's provided photos and text for a number of books. Two of them, *Plants of Northern BC* and *Plants of the Southern Interior* (Lone Pine Publishing), were among the first in BC to be written in easy-to-read layman's language. The first book is in its seventh printing. In 2004, Anna and Gina prepared a

Along with being one of BC's noted naturalists, Anna Roberts is well known for her unique pottery.

guide to ants in the local grasslands and forests. When butterflies caught her attention, Anna compiled a list of the seventy-two species common to this area, along with their host plants, and where and when they can be found. The information and photographs were included in *Butterflies of British Columbia*, published by UBC press in 2001. Along with sharing information through books and guides, Anna conducts field tours and workshops, using the Cariboo Chilcotin landscape as her classroom. Every year for the last fifty years (most recently at Elder College) she has taught adult classes on natural history subjects.

Her work has not gone unnoticed. She is a lifetime member of the Field Naturalists, and has received numerous awards, including the prestigious McTaggart-Cowan Outstanding Naturalist Award, which she received in May 2011 in recognition of her many contributions toward "increasing awareness and understanding of the world of nature." It was presented by John Neville, president of BC Nature, at the BC Nature Conference on the Williams Lake campus of Thompson Rivers University.

Along with her work in the natural word, Anna is one of the Cariboo's foremost potters. She'd been potting for years when she found some places with good pottery-making clay, and in the early 1960s she began working with it. She's continued to dig her own clay. "It's satisfying being intimately involved in every stage, even though it takes so much time and energy," she explains.

In the mid-1960s, after local artist Vivien Cowan held a successful pottery workshop in the Sugar Cane community, she and the workshop leader talked Anna into organizing a workshop for the general public. There was so much interest they held two sessions. Attendees formed the Cariboo Potters Guild, which is still going strong.

In 1977 Kim built his mother a studio overlooking the lake. In recent years she has displayed her work for a few days each fall for the public to come and look or buy. She donates pieces to fundraisers and is known for her original centerpieces for banquets.

Her pottery is distinctive. The wonderful surface impressions reflect her love of nature. She treats the surface of her pots in ways that accentuate line and proportions and allow the unique colours of the clay to show. A specialty is burnished-ware, made by mixing two different coloured clays then rubbing the partly dried clay with an agate to give a shiny surface.

"When making high-fired vases or planters I usually only glaze the inside, leaving the outside the red or brown colour of the local clay," she says. She doesn't use a wheel, preferring to hand-throw her pieces.

Anna's interest in nature hasn't been restricted to wildlife. Shortly after they moved to South Lakeside, John bought a horse, a high-spirited thoroughbred. Anna would ride in the early mornings before the family was up. She also rode in stampede parades with friend Gwen

Anna has written a number of books. Her latest is a guide to the Williams Lake River Valley, which she co-authored with ecologist Ordell Steen. She took all the pictures. Photo: Stephen Walker.

Ringwood. "The parades were all horses and foot traffic then, no big trucks," Anna recalls. "We rode with the Trail Riders."

Music is another part of Anna's life. When she was eleven, her parents started her on cello lessons, and she played with groups during high school. She played with a local group in Williams Lake for some years, mostly for their own enjoyment, but they also played for the medieval market a few times.

Anna travels extensively, usually with her sister. The two have visited the Arctic, the Galapagos, South America, the USA, and BC's west coast. They go somewhere different every year.

Anna feels a strong connection between the spiritual and natural worlds. She is a long-time member of St. Andrews United Church where she enjoys attending worship services. "They nourish my relationship with God," she says.

Anna's latest book, *A field guide to the Williams Lake River Valley*, written with ecologist Ordell Steen, was self-published and is being sold at the Nature Centre. The profits from the book are being donated to the Williams Lake Field Naturalists. Anna has provided all the photographs.

June Striegler

Over Seventy Years Teaching

As June Day stood surveying the one-room, log-cabin school at Springhouse on an October morning in 1940, she had no idea she was starting on a path that would take her to the far corners of the globe in a career that spanned over seventy years.

June Day was raised in Canoe, BC, on the Shuswap Lake. Fresh from Victoria Normal School, she'd had a long, arduous journey by Canadian Pacific Railway boat, ferry and Pacific Great Eastern Railway train to reach Williams Lake, but it was just the first of many trips in a life that would find her still teaching on her ninety-first birthday.

Teaching was not June's first choice. She wanted to be an archeologist, but the Depression years didn't leave much latitude for girls to continue their schooling. Making a living was of more importance, so for seventy-eight dollars a month, she found herself at Springhouse in the Williams Lake area. It was here she began to appreciate the need for a flexible approach to education, an approach she continued to develop over the years. Summarized, it would go something like this: "It isn't what you put into your head that counts, but what you take out."

After a year and a half at Springhouse, June was appointed principal to the three-room school at Clinton. She is believed to be the first female principal in the Cariboo. She met and married Bob Striegler, a cowboy and ranch hand. Their elder son, Bruce, was born and June "thankfully" (according to her) gave up teaching, which she thought was forever. However, when Bruce was a year old, a trip to Vanderhoof to visit Bob's family resulted in June spending a year teaching there.

The next stop was 100 Mile House where for several years Bob was ranch foreman for Lord Martin Cecil. June had ample opportunity to polish her equestrian skills. A move to the Cotton Ranch at Riske Creek resulted in more outdoor time in between cooking and looking after the house. When Bob found her kicking a dead, unplucked chicken around the kitchen he realized she had an intense dislike of cooking, and he suggested she go back to teaching. In the fall of 1954 the family, which now included son Ken, settled in Alexis Creek. She taught there until 1957 when the school board offered her a choice of two jobs, principal at Glendale or Lac La Hache. She chose Lac La Hache and was there for sixteen years.

The Lac La Hache population was growing, and the old two-room school became inadequate, so the school district built a new school. The opening was delayed for various reasons, but June and the children moved in anyway. When the time came for the official opening sometime later, as June was handed the golden key she said, much to everyone's amusement, "Well, this will be better than coming in the window."

In 1973 June moved to the 150 Mile school as principal. About fifty percent of the children there were Shuswap, Chilcotin and Carrier who boarded at St. Joseph's Mission. June's mandate was to effect integration between the white people and First Nations. "That in itself wasn't too difficult," June says, "but the infighting between the tribal groups did create some interesting times."

During her three years there, June become active in the BC Teachers' Federation and for several years she served on the North Central District Council. She was a Project Teach instructor, and a member of the Professional Development Associate Group, which travelled all over BC giving workshops and designing workshops intended to help classroom teachers. She continued her involvement with the professional organization and was president of the local group when she retired. She was a founding member of the Cariboo Chilcotin Retired Teachers' Association and continues as a member of three provincial committees.

In June 1976, June moved to Williams Lake as principal of Marie Sharpe School. After four years there she moved to Poplar Glade. Bob, who had been failing in health for some time, died at this time. Through her professional organization, June was offered an opportunity to become part of Project Overseas, a joint effort of Canadian International Development Agency (CIDA) and the Canadian Teachers' Federation (CTF). In the summer of 1981 she went to Ghana as part of a team working with the Ghanian teachers in reading techniques. The next year she returned to lead a team working with superintendents and principals with a view to improving teacher training.

She found the Ghanian culture interesting. "The British left Ghana with paved roads, TVs and telephones, but with no infrastructure in place. Things were rapidly falling apart. Schools in the rural areas were often nothing more than metal roofs supported on poles, with dirt floors," she recalls. "There was little money for school supplies and teachers became very innovative. At one time they improvised a globe out of breadfruit shell with details painted on."

When June arrived home from Ghana, it was to prepare for a new adventure. This came about when the manager at Gibraltar Mines asked if she could recommend someone to teach the children of the mine executives at Marcropper Mine on Marindugue Island in the Philippines. June recommended herself. She took a year's leave of absence from Poplar Glade, negotiated a salary, and was off to the Philippines, via Japan and Hong Kong.

She went for one year and stayed seven. She loved the country and the people and really enjoyed her job. As well as teaching and supervising the school for the mine executives' children, she served as liaison for two Filipino schools supported by the mine. June lived in the mine compound with the staff, but she went to the barrio for visits, parties and celebrations, and shopped in the local markets. She got to know many of the local people and, at the age of sixty-two, she learned to play golf.

June Striegler's teaching career has taken her to Africa and the Philippines, but she's also travelled to many other countries. Here she is in Cairo, Egypt.

"That was one of the recreations offered at the mine site. Along with tennis courts, a bowling alley, and an excellent swimming pool, all of which we could use for the school sports," she says.

As a youngster, she dreamed of travelling to faraway places, although, as a child of the Depression, such ideas were only dreams. She had a list of sights to see: The Great Wall of China, Egyptian pyramids, Hadrian's Wall, Taj Mahal, Mt. Everest, Borabadur Temple (Java), Ayres Rock, Stonehenge and Delphi (Greece). Part of her salary was a ticket home once a year, and since the Philippines is almost halfway around the world, it was possible for her to visit all these and many other places enroute. She's been around the world several times and has visited over fifty different countries. Travelling continues to be a large part of her life.

When all the children at the Marindugue Island school were ready to go on to higher education, June came home. She had retired from Poplar Glade, but just before she left the Philippines, a call came from Ottawa. The political situation in Liberia, West Africa, was exceedingly volatile, she was told. The CTF wanted an experienced leader to take a team to Monrovia to deal with teaching methods. Would she go? She would.

In December 1982 she set out once again for West Africa. While the team was there, the civil war started, so it was an uneasy time. The team members went home in January, but June stayed on to work on teacher evaluation with a team from the University of Liberia.

Then she retired again. While vacationing in Mexico, she received a call from Gene Bare, Assistant Superintendent of Schools in Williams Lake. There was a problem at the Tatla Lake school, in the Chilcotin country, he said. Would June help out? It sounded interesting so she was off again on what proved to be another career, troubleshooting for School District #27. After Tatla Lake there was a need for an English and social studies teacher at Columneetza Secondary School in Williams Lake. Once again, June went there for one year and stayed for nearly seven. Towards the end of that time the principal at the remote Nemiah school in the Chilcotin left unexpectedly, and June was called in to finish the term. Nemiah is a beautiful place, and the school is a community school with lots of parent involvement. "I knew most of the parents. I'd taught them at the 150," June explains. She enjoyed her time there and when the band council asked her to stay the next year, she did.

In 2000, when June was eighty years old, the school district asked her to take the principal's job at Crescent Heights. The school was slated to be closed and the superintendent didn't see any point in giving the principal's job to someone for one or two years. After that, June retired again, but soon she became involved with the Cariboo Chilcotin Partners for Literacy, a non-profit group that works with adults in the community. Since 2001, she's been the co-coordinator of the Partner Assisted

Learning Programme (PAL), working with adults at the Williams Lake campus of the Thompson Rivers University. Her students range from eighteen to eighty years of age. She works one-to-one with students and holds workshops for the volunteer tutors. The program goes all year round but June takes August off, although she keeps in touch with what is happening.

"People feel worthless, and suddenly they see the light. Sometimes it is young people who need a little boost to get into university. Helping people find ways around problems, seeing the self-confidence they get when they can learn, is worth more than any amount of money," June says. She believes in teaching people to learn. She says there isn't any point in having knowledge if you can't use it. And she likes working "outside the system."

Over the years, June was prepared to take on whatever challenges the school district offered her, but she has a low tolerance for unacceptable behaviour and she has had no qualms whatsoever about ruffling feathers. She has strong opinions accompanied by a wry sense of humour, and the latter often catches people off guard.

Despite a life filled with teaching and helping others, June says she has never been a do-gooder. "There are great rewards for me in what I do. If other people benefit, that is good (too)."

Ethel Winger

Political Pioneer and Gold Prospector

*E*thel Winger is not only a political pioneer; she is also one of the few women in the province who actively prospects for gold.

Until she was elected mayor in 1983, politics in Williams Lake was mostly a man's game. And until she was chosen to chair the Cariboo Regional District Board two years later, regional politics were also dominated by men.

She comes by the pioneering spirit naturally. Her father, Tom Kinvig, came to the Cariboo in 1917 and started a freight business, hauling mail, freight and passengers to mines at the Bullion Pit and Quesnel Forks from the 153 Mile. Tom did some mining, ran some cattle, and built and operated the Keithley Creek Hotel and store. The hotel catered to the many bachelors who worked in the bush gold mines in the area, but along with the miners, hotel visitors included tourists, mining engineers, politicians and even movie stars. Many of the miners played instruments and there were some grand parties in the "snake room" (the hotel lounge).

Ethel's mother, Melva, who racked up a few firsts of her own, was chief cook and housekeeper, looking after the hotel's thirteen rooms, bar, store and dining room, a big garden, and two small daughters. Ethel was born at the hotel, and she and her sister Beatrice spent their early years there. They were the darlings of the miners, who gave them a lot of attention.

When the Kinvigs sold the hotel, Tom focused on packing supplies to the five

While attending high school in Quesnel, Ethel Kinvig (Winger) was crowned Ice Capades Queen—even though she didn't know how to skate.

mines operating in the Yanks Peak area. Melva became a freighter too, making many trips on her own. She was an excellent teamster, and when Tom bought the first freight truck to travel the rough, old Keithley Creek wagon road, she drove that too. She was the Cariboo's first women "trucker," making the weekly 125-kilometre trip from Keithley Creek to Williams Lake.

Ethel attended school in many places. She boarded at Miocene for Grades 1 and 2, then spent two years at Likely. The family was living in Keithley Creek when Melva broke her leg, and Ethel went home and was homeschooled for four years. The next stops were Merritt for Grade 9, Williams Lake for Grade 10, and Quesnel for two years to take secretarial and commercial courses that weren't offered in Williams Lake.

Along the way, she was on every student council possible. She was July Queen in Merritt and Ice Capades Queen in Quesnel (even though she couldn't skate). One event in Quesnel changed her life—she met Dave Winger on a blind date.

She graduated in 1953, returned to Williams Lake and went to work for the law firm Skipp and Cade. Dave followed her and they married in 1955. Ethel would soon become Mrs. Mom, looking after their three children, Vern, Wesley and Debra. She was involved in everything they did, including hockey, figure skating, the Cariboo Music Festival and the 4H Club. She was active in the PTA and helped found the town's first kindergarten. On the side she canvassed for the Red Cross, Heart Fund, Cancer Fund, the BC Kidney Foundation, and whatever and whoever needed her.

"I volunteered for everything, and I really gave business people a pain," she recalls. She did so much soliciting for funds people would hide when they saw her coming because they thought she was looking for donations. She also worked part-time in the office at the Williams Lake and Quesnel cattle sales for the BC Livestock Association for several years.

She went back to work full-time for two reasons. Dave later went into a partner-ship in Broadway Rentals, but before that he was a bricklayer and stonemason. Jobs were scarce in the winter, and an extra paycheque would come in handy. The other reason was that her family and friends were giving her a bad time because they said she was overdoing the "mother" bit. She worked for lawyer Tom Rhodes, and then for the Skipp, Vanderburg and Darcy law firm.

She began her career in municipal government in 1972 when she took the job as secretary to town council under the leadership of Mayor Jim Fraser. That led to the position of Acting Deputy Clerk, then Assistant Administrator for six years. The town was booming in the early 1970s. Gibraltar Mines had opened, the mills were going full tilt, and ranches were thriving. Williams Lake was the centre for both provincial and federal regional offices and there was a lot of development going on. Many dignitaries, including Prime Minister Trudeau and Prince Philip, came to visit. Premier Dave Barrett was invited to open the stampede and he not only came, he brought his entire cabinet. It was a busy and exciting time.

Ethel resigned from her job at city hall in the fall of 1979 and enrolled in the real estate sales program. Within a month she was recruited by the Cariboo Regional District as Interim Administrator. At the time, the management of the (CRD) was pretty rocky but until a new administrator could be hired, she helped bring the bylaws up to date, assisted the board in their duties and helped establish a good working relationship between all staff. When she finished her real estate course, she listed and sold properties from Bella Coola, McLeese Lake, Horsefly and Williams Lake for three years for Murray Hume Agencies.

In 1983 she was talked into running for mayor against incumbent Tom Mason and Councillor Gurbax Saini. She had an advantage in that she knew the inner workings of the city and she won handily.

"I never was a politician," she says. "I just like to get things done." Getting in-volved in city politics was a way to do that. Her motto is, if it's worth doing, do it right, and while she didn't make everyone happy, she always did what she thought was right.

One of her campaign promises was "no hidden taxation for pet projects." When the Glendale community joined Williams Lake, city council allocated the provincial money it received to build a new city hall. Ethel inherited the construction and she was concerned about spending $1.2 million on building when there were no washrooms in Kiwanis Park and no sidewalks in Glendale. She kept a close eye on spending during her two terms in office.

At the time, there didn't seem to be much cooperation between the Cariboo municipalities and the rural regional district directors on the CRD. Ethel believed she could improve things, and in 1985 she ran for, and was elected, as CRD Chair, replacing the incumbent. She called the CRD position a "dubiously prestigious seat" and she had one word in response to those who wondered how she would have time to head both the city and the CRD governments. The word was "delegate." It took time to resolve all the issues. It took time to rebuild trust between staff, volunteers and Victoria, but Ethel's philosophy of "if it needs to be done, do it" paid off.

With the goal of having full communications and community participation, Ethel had an open-door policy both at the town and the CRD. She named a number of new committees to increase efficiency and get the community working together. She got the ownership of the Stampede Grounds nailed down, worked with the women's centre, labour council, recreation and arts groups, and named a manager of business development. She made the arena committee a standing committee of the CRD instead of a sub-committee. Among the highlights during her first term as mayor were Rick Hansen's homecoming after his Man in Motion tour, and the establishment of the Alex Fraser Research Centre.

Dave, Ethel's best friend and loving husband, died unexpectedly in 1985, just a few months before the civic election. She was pressured into running again and won a second term. She says she didn't really have time to think it through, or she might not have done it. The second term had some highlights, including Expo 86. Ethel was with the Williams Lake delegation to the world's fair. They all wore blue cowboy

Ethel divides her time between her home in Williams Lake and her cabin at Keithley Creek, where she pans for gold. She enjoys her ATV in the summer and snowmobiling in winter.

hats. She also served as director of the Northern Development Council, director of the North Central Municipal Association and director of the Cariboo Thompson Library Association.

She lost the 1987 election to Ray Woods. She says she enjoyed the "wonderful experience" in city politics, and made many lifelong friends. Her next career was as a realtor at Northern Realty, and then MP Dave Worthy asked her to manage Community Futures. She says she didn't know much about the latter but the community knew less.

"That was both interesting and rewarding work," Ethel recalls. "We had five excellent staff and we were able to help hundreds of small businesses get started with counselling and small loans up to $75,000. We were very successful in helping hard-working entrepreneurs and in keeping our losses to a minimum."

When Ethel retired in 1996 she really retired, both from paid employment and volunteer work. Except for the Regional Resources Board (which rarely meets) she doesn't sit on any boards, nor does she do any fundraising. She still does some "unattached" volunteer work. "I believe my family suffered when I was so busy," she says. "So now I have time for them."

She makes her home at Terra Ridge in Williams Lake but spends five or six months at her second home at Keithley Creek on the original Kinvig homestead. Her children have vacation homes nearby and her grandchildren spend most of the summer there, exploring the countryside in all-terrain vehicles. In the winter they like to snowmobile.

Although the Keithley Creek area has been thoroughly mined, there are still bits and pieces of gold here and there and since she retired Ethel has had time for recreational prospecting. She works two claims that have been in her family for over sixty years. She started by doing assessment work for her dad and got hooked.

She also travels. Most years she goes on a major trip, often a cruise. When she's home she plays bridge at least twice a week, and spends a lot of time with her family. "I feel very fortunate to have lived my life in Williams Lake and in the beautiful Cariboo," Ethel says. "The people are fantastic. I have an absolutely great, loving family and I feel grateful for the many varied experiences offered to this country girl."

Gloria Atamanenko

The Cariboo is Home

The Atamanenkos' home on Tuffy Springs Ranch near 150 Mile House sits on high ground with an unobstructed view in all directions. In the early morning, their dining room window frames the sun rising over the hills in the east. In the evening, their living room window frames the sun setting behind the hills to the west. The view is one of the reasons they bought the ranch when George retired seventeen years ago. The Atamanenkos were not strangers to the Cariboo. They lived in Williams Lake in the late 1950s before making their home in Victoria and they've had property in the Chilcotin for years. It was a matter of coming home.

Gloria has always been active in community affairs. She suffered a stroke in 2007 that put her in a wheelchair, but not out of action, and she keeps her helping hand out to the community.

Gloria is the daughter of Ukrainian immigrants who settled in the Fort Vermillion area in Northern Alberta in the 1930s. The homesteads were few and far between. The winters were long and cold, the summer's growing season short. Times were tough in the Depression years and Gloria grew up doing her share of the farm work. Her parents were anxious for her to further her education (and so was she) and after completing Grade 8 in the one-room local school, she went to the Eastern Seaboard in the US to stay with an uncle for high school. It was there she first experienced racism in the attitudes toward the black community.

Gloria did well in school and won a scholarship to a Quaker college where she studied to be a social worker, but before she graduated, her uncle became ill. She left school to look after him, and got a job as a social worker that included in-service training. When her uncle died in 1954, she went home "as a place to start from."

Alberta's welfare services required social workers to have a university degree, and an official suggested Gloria go to BC where a degree wasn't necessary. In the meantime, she met George, a land inspector, who was friends with a neighbour. They became interested in each other, and decided they both would try BC. George landed a job in Williams Lake, and Gloria found one in Vancouver. She loved the coastal city but it wasn't too handy for the romance. She managed to transfer to Williams Lake, and she and George were married in 1957. Their son Boris was born at Williams Lake, and along the way they fell in love with the Chilcotin country. They bought property at Horn Lake and spent as much time as they could there.

Gloria's job included visiting elderly prospectors in the Likely, Keithley Creek and Horsefly areas. Most of them lived in cabins well off the road, and without the help of one of her clients, she says she might never have found them. Some were still prospecting, still hoping to find their fortune. Gloria has written their story, "Aging

Although she is now confined to a wheelchair, Gloria Atamanenko hasn't given up her interest in growing things. She's been donating seedlings to the Scout Island Nature Centre's spring fundraiser for years.

on the Gold Rush Trail," for *Lived Experiences*, a literary magazine published by Van Andruss of Lillooet.

A series of events led George to leave land inspecting and go into land-use planning. They moved to Vancouver where he attended the University of British Columbia for what was then a new program. He was awarded a scholarship, and after finishing the two-year program, he went to work in Victoria. Son Peter was born there. Gloria went back to social work, and back to school. The University of Victoria didn't have a master's program for social work at the time, so she took her master's degree in counselling.

Gloria has spent most of her adult life fighting for the rights and comfort of children and the learning disabled, but she had a difficult time with what she calls the "new" attitudes in social work. The bureaucracy and politics got her down. Being a rebel at heart, and an outspoken one to boot, she often found herself at odds with her superiors. The final straw came one day when a supervisor asked whose side she was on—"ours or theirs."

"I was on 'their' side, the clients' side. I thought that was what social work was all about," Gloria says, still indignant that it might be otherwise. "I went home and cried over the potatoes while I cooked supper and then said to hell with them."

The Atamanenkos lived in the provincial capital for twenty-five years but they didn't lose their connection with the Cariboo. They visited the property at Horn Lake every chance they had, and always felt part of the Chilcotin community. "We loved to hike and camp, and we love the people," Gloria says. "We were free to enjoy life there."

When George retired, Gloria says they didn't really come back to the Cariboo, as they felt they'd never been away. It didn't take them long to get involved in local activities. George has a long-time interest in heritage and local history. Gloria became involved with the Learning Disabilities Association, and was on the board of the Skills Centre. She is a strong supporter of Scout Island and was actively involved in fundraising, particularly providing seedlings (she was known for her tomato plants) for the spring fundraiser. She is an excellent cook, and always took goodies to events and to the homebound and ill, as well as ethnic dishes to the Kiwanis' International dinners.

And she writes. She was a force behind *Gumption and Grit* (Caitlin Press), the first book on Cariboo Chilcotin women, published in 2009. She's written a number of pieces for *Lived Experiences*, and she translated "14 Months on Franz Joseph Land" the story of Ukrainian scientist Mykhallo Ivanychuk's exploration of the High Arctic, published in 2002.

As for community work, Gloria is active in the Council of Canadians and the NDP, and from her wheelchair she has her hand and her heart out to whoever needs comforting.

Satwant Johal

The Stars Are the Same Everywhere

When Satwant Johal visited Tibet a few years ago, she was duly impressed with the Himalayas, but she says they can't compare with our own mountains in Bella Coola and Tatlayoko. "We have everything here," she says.

Satwant is best known for her twenty-six years as a cook at Cariboo Lodge. The lodge, which closed in 2004, was a government-operated residential care facility in Williams Lake. She enjoyed working there and she was a favourite of the residents. "It was a comfortable place to work," she says.

Satwant was born in Port Montgomery in the Punjab province. In 1947, when the British Colony of India was partitioned, part of the province was divided between India and Pakistan. Satwant's father, a farmer, lost property to Pakistan and he never really got over the shock. Satwant is the second-youngest daughter from his second marriage. There were twelve children altogether, and all were educated. Satwant trained as a teacher and speaks three languages.

When she was growing up, Satwant said she was always rebelling. On the farm she tried to do what she wanted to do, and she objected so much to the tradition of a bride's dowry that she didn't want to get married. Her mother encouraged her to stand up for herself and she always has. Her mother also said she didn't have to have an arranged marriage if she didn't want to, but when a cousin suggested a young man for her, Satwant had second thoughts. "I was very fond of the cousin and I trusted her, and in the end I agreed," she says.

Satwant and her friend Viday Prenjat in 1964 on Satwant's rooftop in India. Both were school-teachers.

Surjit was working in England and had come home seeking a bride. Satwant saw only his picture before the wedding. After their marriage they went to England.

Satwant and Surjit came to Williams Lake in the early 1970s. They were living in England when they made the move. They had three small children, twins Harjit and Gary, and baby Angela. Surjit was an educator and had a good job, but members of Satwant's family had come to Canada earlier, and the Johals liked what they heard about it.

"We had a good lifestyle, but we were young, we wanted to see new places," Satwant explains. Her mother, Tejwant, who lived with them, wasn't keen on the move but she didn't fuss. "The stars are the same everywhere," she said.

They went first to New Westminster, then Satwant, her mother and the babies came on the bus to join her brother, Ranjit Sandhu, in Williams Lake. Surjit stayed in New Westminster to get his first aid ticket, then joined them.

One of Satwant's first surprises in Canada was the casual dress. "Everyone in England dressed up, but here everyone was comfortable."

Surjit didn't have a trade, so he took whatever came along while going to night school to upgrade. An on-call job at the P&T Mill eventually led to full-time employment. The Johals had an agreement with Ranjit; he paid the rent, they bought the food. Their first home wasn't much of a place. It leaked when it rained and there

Satwant's travels have included a visit to Tibet. She loved the people and found the countryside interesting, but she believes nothing can compare to the beauty of the Cariboo Chilcotin.

were nails sticking up in the floor, which was not good with a crawling baby.

Satwant's first job was washing dishes at the Bil Nor restaurant. It was a fair hike down the highway but Satwant walked to work. She says the restaurant owner, Bill Gillis, was good to work for, and after a year he asked her to take on the job of cooking. She was at the Bil Nor for four years, and trained a number of South Asian girls who couldn't speak English.

When the finances got better, the Johals bought a duplex in downtown Williams Lake on Barnard Street. Satwant cooked at the Travelodge, Chilcotin Inn and Homesteader before going to Cariboo Lodge in 1977. All was well with the family, but it wasn't to last. In September of that year, Satwant, Surjit and the children set out for Vancouver early on a weekend morning. Satwant was driving when she felt something wasn't right with the car, so Surjit took the wheel. Just before Lytton, the vehicle went out of control, jumped over a guardrail, and plunged down a four-hundred-foot cliff. Satwant doesn't remember too much about the accident itself, except that people came to help right away, and given the steep incline it was a difficult rescue. They were taken to Lytton Hospital where she and the children were treated for bumps and bruises. Surjit, however, died of his injuries.

Satwant and her friend Leet Meuller relax in the Tatlayoko valley, surrounded by some of BC's more spectacular mountains.

"He was such a good man, such a good father," Satwant says. "I didn't know what to do without him." She thought about returning to India but a neighbour told her, "Don't go back to India, whatever you do." She heeded that advice.

In the first months after his death she had some anxious times, but she was surprised at the help and comfort she received from so many people. "I'd only been here seven years. I didn't know so many people cared," she says.

The IWA (woodworkers union) helped her find what help was available, like the widow's pension and other types of aid she didn't know about. There was no personal life insurance, but there was thirty thousand dollars from the mill. She said it felt wrong to take money from a death, but it did allow her to buy the home on Pigeon Avenue where she still lives. She sold the duplex.

Cariboo Lodge was operated by a non-profit organization. The salaries it could afford to pay weren't enough to support a family, and there were no benefits. When Satwant went back to work, the Lodge staff were discussing pay and working conditions, and she got involved, and it meant going to endless meetings.

"Sometimes I just had to go home," Satwant recalls. The staff chose to join a union, and then, she says, "things were so much better."

Satwant left the Lodge before it was closed by Interior Health, and she is one of the many who wondered at the wisdom of the closing. She was involved in making sure the staff was looked after.

Satwant had little time to socialize when the children were young, but when she was in her forties she decided to see more of the world, including the local countryside. She hiked all over the place, visited Tatlayoko and Bella Coola, and everywhere she could. Her travels abroad have convinced her just how beautiful this country is.

Satwant's focus now is to keep healthy, and she walks and swims. She is involved with several groups, including the seniors' centre. She attends the Community Church, where she says there is a good mix of people. She spends a lot of time with family and friends. Harjit and Angela are in Vancouver, Gary works at Gibraltar Mine, and she now has two grandchildren.

Satwant never did lose her rebellious nature, and to this day if she feels something is wrong, she gets involved to fix it.

3

MAKING THEIR MARK

The Bayliff Women

Making History in the Chilcotin

Provincial Court Judge Elizabeth Bayliff is the fourth generation in a Chilcotin pioneer Bayliff family. Much has been recorded about the Bayliff men, but little about the women in the family. Elizabeth's great-grandfather, Hugh Bayliff, was one of the British gentry who came to the Cariboo in the 1880s seeking land, not gold, and he found what he was looking for at the west end of the Chilcotin Valley. He established the Chilancoh Ranch near Redstone in 1887 and what began as a 160-acre pre-emption in the wilderness is now one of the larger family-owned ranches in the Cariboo Chilcotin. It is one of the earliest ranches in the Chilcotin country, and one of the few "Century" ranches in BC, a title given farms and ranches that have stayed in the same family for one hundred years.

Hugh visited England in 1888 and returned with a bride, Gertrude Tyndle. She was one of the first white women on the vast Chilcotin plateau. She joined Mrs. Tom Hance (Nellie) at Hanceville and Augustine Franklin at what is now the Gang Ranch, both at the east end of the valley. Gertrude's father was the editor of the *London Times*. Her gracious London lifestyle can't have prepared her for the primitive life in the Chilcotin, but in some ways the Chilcotin lifestyle adapted to her. She turned Hugh's little log cabin into an island of Edwardian England in the wilderness. She brought linen, silver and fine china with her from London, and she didn't pack them away, she used them. Everyone dressed for dinner. She never

Hugh Bayliff's log cabin in the wilderness was transformed into a picture of Edwardian England when Gertrude arrived from London, England. She brought her city lifestyle with her.

lowered her standards, although one issue was a draw. The floors in the cabin were rough whip-sawn boards and the cracks between them broke the heels off all her London city shoes.

Gertrude knew a bit about medicine, and that was useful, as the bachelors in the country tended to treat any ailment or injury with coal oil. She was also an excellent horsewoman (side-saddle) and that too was useful as she helped with the cattle round-ups. The Bayliffs always had good horses, which were brought over from England. In the early 1900s, when the Chilcotin valley was more populated, there were annual race meets at Bechers Prairie. Gertrude participated in the races and she usually brought home trophies. They built a new home, a series of log structures joined by an open verandah.

Their one son, Gabriel (Gay), was born in 1898. They sent him to England for schooling at an early age, and he returned to the old country later to fight in World War I. He married Dorothy Dyson in 1923. Dorothy was the daughter of Colonel and Mrs. Louis Dyson. Mrs. Dyson's brother, Reginald Newton, had the ranch neighbouring the Bayliffs. Dorothy made several visits to the Newtons, her first when she was eight years old, travelling by stagecoach. She remembered being frightened when she was told to get out and walk while the horses struggled up the major hills. She was afraid the coach would go off and leave her alone in the wilderness. She made her second trip a few years later in the first car to make its way into the Chilcotin.

Dorothy was affectionately called "Missus" by family and friends, and was dearly loved by everyone. She maintained the gracious lifestyle while doing her share of cowboying. She was an excellent horsewoman and like Gertrude, she helped with the cattle roundups. She had a Chinese cook, but in those days there were large hay crews to feed and not too many modern conveniences. The current Bayliff home was built later of lumber milled at the ranch. It took six years to build, and Missus and Gay were in the process of moving into it in October 1925 when son Tim arrived. Missus always said it was moving a particularly heavy box of books that brought on her labour. She and Gay had two sons, Tim and Tony.

Merle Glenny was the third chatelaine at the Chilancoh Ranch. She married Tim, who took over management of the ranch from his father. Merle was a nurse from Somerset, England, who came to Canada with another nurse for what was to be a two-year adventure. Her first job was working out of Regina, serving northern Saskatchewan communities. She was a trained midwife and made trips, sometimes by plane, sometimes by canoe, to deliver babies in the remote communities. She loved this work. Her

Merle Glenny became the third Mrs. Bayliff at Chilancoh Ranch when she married Tim, the oldest son of Gay and Dorothy Bayliff. Merle was also a registered nurse from England.

last job took her to Alexis Creek in 1953 as relief manager at the Red Cross Outpost Hospital. She met Tim when he came to the hospital to have a piece of metal removed from his eye. She wouldn't do it, telling him to go to Williams Lake. He was ticked off because he didn't want to go to Williams Lake. The next meeting must have been friendlier because they were married in the spring of 1954. By then ranches were becoming mechanized, and Merle wasn't required to cowboy or to go on cattle drives. She had her hands full with three children, Elizabeth, Hugh and James, and a big garden.

Tony Bayliff inherited the Newton Ranch from his aunt, Kathleen Newton. He and Barrie Boucher were married in 1962. Barrie has a master's degree in social work, but there wasn't much work in that department in the Chilcotin in the 1970s, so she went to the University of Victoria to get her teacher's training. She taught at the Alexis Creek elementary school for twenty years. Barrie and Tony had two children, Jane and Michael. Heartbreak came to their family when Jane lost her life in a motor vehicle accident.

Dorothy Dyson, who was affectionately called "Missus" by family and friends, was already familiar with the Chilcotin country when she came from England to marry Gay Bayliff in 1923. She had previously visited her aunt and uncle at the Newton Ranch. They were neighbours of the Bayliffs.

Tony and Barrie now enjoy retirement, and Michael and his wife Colleen have the Newton Ranch. Colleen is from Nova Scotia, and like Merle a generation before her, she came to the Chilcotin as a nurse. She was employed with the federal government to work with First Nations communities in the area. She and Mike were married in 1991 and they have three children, Lane, Sarah and Andrew.

Following family tradition, Tim and Merle's oldest son, Hugh, is the fourth generation at the Chilancoh Ranch. Hugh's wife, Hellen (von Harbou) is the fourth Mrs. Bayliff at Chilancoh Ranch. Hellen was born in Germany and raised in Alberta. She has a degree in anthropology from the University of Lethbridge and attended McGill University. She spent several years working in the Middle East, and has also worked as a nature interpreter at Garibaldi Park, and for the BC government in Social Services. Hellen has followed in the footsteps of the Bayliff women by helping with the ranch work, as well as running the office. The Bayliffs practise sustainable agriculture and the Chilancoh ranch is one of the leaders in raising grass-fed, all natural beef. Along with homeschooling the children, Matthew and Maria, Hellen is working on her master's degree in Environmental Management through Royal Roads University.

Jim, Merle and Tim's second son, was ranching near Redstone when he was killed in an accident, leaving his wife, Marion, and sons, Bryce, seven, and Brent, five. Marion, a rancher in her own right, being raised on her family's ranch in Cache Creek, took over operation of the ranch near Redstone until her boys were older. She now lives in Williams Lake where she has traded her western saddle in favour of dressage. She has a boarding stable and hosts a variety of equine events.

Elizabeth was the first daughter in the Bayliff line, and she broke tradition by leaving the ranch to become a lawyer. Growing up, she did all the ranch duties, and she says she thought she did well with riding and handling cattle, but wasn't much good at machinery. She took her early schooling at a one-room school,

Poplar Grove, on the Chezacut Road near Redstone. The two Ross brothers who ranched at Redstone had very large families and their children made up most of the student population. Elizabeth and, later, her brothers were driven to school, sometimes by a teacher who boarded nearby. Elizabeth remembers cramming into a tiny Volkswagen that didn't seem to have any heat. It was a perishingly cold ride with a little peek-hole thawed in the windshield. "It seemed like one endless winter," she recalls.

By the time she was ready for Grade 5, her parents weren't happy with some of the habits she was picking up at school and they sent her to a friend's in Vancouver for what Elizabeth remembers as two years of

Hellen von Harbou and her husband, Hugh Bayliff, are the fourth generation at the historic Chilancoh Ranch. Hellen was born in Germany but raised in Alberta. The Bayliffs practise sustainable agriculture, and raise grass-fed beef. Hellen is fully involved in the ranch operation and that includes doing the office work and marketing. She describes herself as "general ranch hand and problem solver."

misery. She was homesick all the time, but she thinks now it was a good experience. In 1967 she fell off a horse and her injuries kept her in Vancouver General Hospital for months. When she came home she was homeschooled. The next year, Merle moved to Williams Lake with the three children while they went to school during the week and went home weekends.

Elizabeth went to Williams Lake Junior Secondary, graduated from Columneetza in 1973, and went to the University of British Columbia for the Honours English progam. She travelled in Europe after graduating, spending most of the time in France. Her intention was to become bilingual. When she came home, she worked in Williams Lake as a teller at the Bank of Commerce, then went to Prince Rupert where she worked as a legal secretary. That work convinced her to become a lawyer, and she enrolled at Queen's University in Kingston, Ontario, for the three-year law program. She articled in Williams Lake and was called to the bar in 1984. She practised in Williams Lake, and then in Prince George for eleven years. She practised in Quesnel for two years before being appointed as Provincial Court Judge in 2001, and she came home again to Williams Lake.

One thing is for certain. The Bayliff women, along with the Bayliff men, will continue to play an important role both in the social and the economic welfare of the Cariboo Chilcotin country.

Marg Evans

What We Have on Earth is Worth Cherishing

For over a decade, Marg Evans has been managing director of the Cariboo Chilcotin Conservation Society. The society is dedicated to "maintaining and enhancing the quality of the environment as the basis of a strong economy and vital society." Marg has been dedicated to doing that all her adult life.

Born in New Westminster, BC, Marg grew up watching the bush and forest around her home become a busy neighbourhood. She attended New Westminster Secondary School, where she had a strong interest in music, particularly saxophone, guitar and the piano. She took singing lessons in elementary school, and joined musical theatre in high school. In 1970 she entered Simon Fraser University (SFU) with an arts and science background and a strong interest in the outdoors and human character and psychology. She enrolled in the environmental education program SFU was developing. "We were the guinea pigs," Marg says, "a group of about thirty student teachers."

One of their activities was a snowy trek to McQueen Lake in Kamloops in late November, and on this trip she met Don Evans, her future husband. After their wedding, the two went to Fort St. John, where they lived in an old San Francisco streetcar, cared for locals' dogs, and worked with street kids. The streetcar was heated by an old wood cookstove that didn't keep the temperature warm enough to thaw the snow tracked in on the floor. Temperatures dipped to minus sixty-five. On the plus side, Marg says they experienced the "wonder of the deep winter nights and northern lights."

They spent the next year at Fort St. James where they taught, did childcare work, canoed and got acquainted with the diverse wildlife of the area. Next they travelled across Canada with two dogs and a cat, having some interesting experiences along the way. Once they almost got caught in the Bay of Fundy tides, and for a time they lived in a lighthouse at Murray Harbour, PEI, where sea lions wallowed and huge lobster claws littered the orange beaches. By January they were homesick and headed back to BC.

They tried city life, Don as a PE coordinator in New Westminster, Marg in a Burnaby community school, but they missed the rural life. In 1977 they came to the Cariboo to teach at Skyline, School District #27's alternate school.

"We loved the central location, and the climate, and the district was open to having an outdoor program," Marg says. "We began by going to the coast and buying six canoes, sets of snowshoes, compasses and guitars."

A number of Marg Evans' jobs involved field work, and she often took her daughters Rikki-Lee (on horseback) and Kiana (in the backpack) with her.

They developed a rotational trip system for the school: canoeing and hiking in the fall, snowshoeing and cross-country skiing in winter, and horseback riding, more hiking and canoe trips in the spring. They had some incredible experiences, including encounters with moose on canoe trips and cross-country skiing in a snowstorm. Marg taught basic guitar to the students and they had many campfire singalongs. They took cameras everywhere, and the classroom was covered in photos.

When Don's high-school-aged cousins, Diane and Taki, came to live with them, they joined the camping and canoe trips. One two-week trip on Quesnel Lake turned out to be particularly eventful. The first eight days were wet and thick with mosquitoes. They were about to give up when the weather improved and they made it to Mitchell River. They were fishing near the beach camp when a huge burbot swam under one of the canoes.

"It was the size of a small shark and gave us a start," Marg says. "Back at camp we were greeted by a skunk family meandering across the beach toward our camp. Fortunately they veered away but I cannot think of how we could have rid the camp of them without dire consequences. A weasel feasted on our sunflower seeds and we watched a bear along the lakeshore as we sailed past. The winds got so high we were forced off for long periods. One day we pitched a tarp between two canoes and sailed, a good rest from paddling."

Marg says she was originally terrified of horses, but riding was an important part of the program. "We began, greener than grass, learning how to ride, then pack, until we spent up to a month at a time exploring the mountains in the Chilcotin."

They were at Skyline for nine years, with one year off to open a one-room, log schoolhouse in Kluskus. Students learned the need to watch the weather and respect wildlife, and this was tested on their final trip, a canoe trip on Horsefly Lake. The weather was miserable, cold and wet. A storm was kicking up whitecaps so they stopped at a small island to take a break.

"When we landed, a couple of the kids explored the island. About five minutes later they streaked out of the woods screaming 'moose!' It was a cow and calf, so we piled into the canoes and back to the storm. The calf came flying out and took off into the water. When the cow emerged, she didn't see her calf, so she took after us," Marg relates. "We yelled for everyone to paddle hard and prayed the calf would bellow from shore. Finally, the mom figured out we didn't have her calf and she headed to shore."

After Skyline, Don opened Evans Training, a horse-training business, and Marg went to work with the Ministry of Environment, Wildlife Branch, on a bighorn sheep predation study, tracking cougar. This involved capturing, re-collaring, tracking kittens, winter moose tracking on snowshoes, and telemetry flights. It wasn't a job for the timid, but Marg sees all her adventures as learning experiences, and tracking and collaring the cougar was definitely that. On her first day the crew set out at 5 a.m. so they could reach the Junction and Deer Park areas at dawn to scout for cougar tracks.

Heavy snow made everything slippery and Marg spent a lot of time picking herself up from falls. When they spotted tracks, she was given a cougar hound on a leash and was dragged through the woods with the dogs sniffing and howling when they picked up a scent. After six hours they treed a cougar. Marg clambered up a twenty-foot embankment with the cougar in a tree above, and as she reached the top, the cougar came flying down from the tree. "It landed twenty feet away from me and was off at a dead run," she says. "It wasn't something I will ever forget."

The moose study looked at the winter range habits of moose in the west Chilcotin. It meant at least three fixed-wing flights a week and daily on-ground tracking on snowshoes. Morning temperatures were often minus twenty, and some afternoons it would be above zero with rain. Moose were plentiful, on any trip Cariboo Flats would have thirty to forty moose feeding or crossing the highway. Marg got stuck in the snow a few times, and once the whole team was caught in a snowstorm. That time the helicopter pilot spotted a road and followed it to the highway then back to the airport.

Marg was next involved with the BC Forestry Association coordinating a women's employment re-entry program. They created a sound and dialogue tape for Highway 97 brochures, and other educational materials.

The cougar study was related to California bighorn sheep populations, and led to Marg working with Dr. Daryll Hebert in 1989. This was another great learning experience, and she could work from home, a bonus as her first child, Rikki-Lee, was born that August. When the baby was eight months old Marg went back to horseback riding, taking the baby in a backpack. As a wildlife viewing coordinator, Marg created signage and viewing management plans for a half-dozen sites in the region. Daughter Kiani was born in August 1993, and Marg often made trips with both girls in tow, along with Don when he was free.

In 1989 Don began a therapy program, K'an Deni Jalih, for First Nations students between the ages of fifteen and twenty-four. He ran this program from a facility built beside their home, while Marg began a three-year translocation of fisher (weasel family) from the Cariboo to the Kootenays. This experience had its moments as the odd fisher escaped and had to be recaptured.

After a lot of research and training, Don turned Evans Training into a canine facility. Dogs now arrive by plane as well as car from across the country. Developing a website and videotaping the work has allowed him to mentor others.

The outdoors aren't the only attraction for Marg. She has been with musical theatre, and the Potter's and Weavers Guild. She took workshops in several pottery styles but focuses on wildlife natural imprints, rather than functional ware. In weaving she is interested especially in tapestry and she creates nature scenes: forests, ocean, beaches and sunsets in various textures of yarn.

Along with music, swimming is a lifetime interest, and Marg has been skin diving in tropical waters and has taken courses in scuba diving. She enjoys being on the water too, especially canoeing and kayaking. The family has a freighter canoe for longer trips. She also likes hiking and she enjoyed cross-country skiing until she injured her knee. She snowshoes but doesn't consider it recreation. "Not after spending one winter snowshoeing three miles in and out of our residence, sometimes sinking thigh deep in the snow!" she says.

Marg views landscaping as an art, with her garden as tapestry. Her Zen (xeriscape) garden is a pleasing space to sit and enjoy the birds, flowers, and the play of shadows and light as the seasons change. The garden is designed so it gives pleasure even in winter and it's low maintenance.

There would be a huge void in her life without animals, Marg says. Along with the horses, cats and dogs, she has learned from wildlife encounters. Living out of town on the fringe of a forest has brought its own experiences. There are often deer, moose, coyotes, bear and the occasional cougar in the neighbourhood.

Don, Marg and Kiani took their old house apart a few years ago and reclaimed much of the material to renovate their barn, which was the previous school, into their new home. The process gave them an appreciation for "making the most of materials you have."

Marg finds her personal serenity with a group of dear friends who practise yoga. The group has been sharing experiences for fifteen years.

Marg's work with the Conservation Society involves a wide range of activities. She supervises three part-time staff who do Water Wise and Waste Wise programs in partnership with the City and Regional District and programs with the Gavin Lake Education Centre. She participates in numerous public processes and programs, and she produces a Parks Guide plus many pamphlets and displays (she is an accomplished photographer). She writes reports, seeks funding, and serves on a number of boards including the Cariboo Chilcotin Beetle Action Coalition. The society networks with other groups and has an active Listserve, which she is in charge of too.

Marg says, "My work has given me a sense of belonging to a humanity with whom I still have hope will eventually come to realize what we've got here on earth is worth cherishing, and what the costs if we don't."

Janis Bell

Not a Job for the Faint of Heart

"The words I live by are 'life's an attitude.' You can have a good one or a bad one, it's the one thing that only you can control no matter what is going on around you," says Janis Bell, Chief Administrative Officer (CAO) of the Cariboo Regional District (CRD). After thirty-four years, Janis finds her work challenging, interesting and most importantly, she enjoys it. Only Area A Director Ted Armstrong has been with the CRD as long as she has.

Janis Bothamley was born in Williams Lake. In 1966, when she was in Grade 1, her family moved to the Kootenays. They returned to the town in 1972 where Janis continued her education. She credits Betty Kahl, a "wonderful teacher" at Columneetza, for setting her on her career path. "I didn't know what I wanted to do after I graduated," she says. "When career preparation week came along, Betty arranged for me to go the CRD."

She was barely back at school when she received a call from the regional district saying an employee had left, and would she like the job starting immediately. The problem was, she hadn't finished Grade 12. Teachers agreed to accelerate her program (she had honours in math and English) and she went to work as the CRD receptionist on June 1, 1978. One day, CRD Chair John Paul asked her if she could take minutes. She thought she could, and that's how she became secretary to the board. From there she moved up the ranks.

The CRD is huge, covering 85,000 square kilometres. The 65,000 constituents are served by twelve rural and four municipal directors (sixteen different fiefdoms). The geography ranges from rainforest to desert plains and everything in between. Each constituency has its own, and often very different, concerns and issues. For instance, South Cariboo residents want more rules and regulations, and Chilcotin residents want fewer.

"Sometimes it takes time to work things out," Janis notes. She has to work toward solutions rather than giving orders, although she says she's given a lot of those over the years too.

"Life's an attitude. You can have a good one or a bad one."

She oversees a staff of 165. Some, like rural librarians, might only work four hours a week. CRD responsibilities include water, sewer, recreation complexes, libraries, streetlights in rural areas, planning, building inspection, garbage and the regional hospital function. The latter funds equipment and other major capital projects. Garbage is a particularly contentious issue. Janis says she isn't an environmentalist but "it's obvious we can't keep burying garbage even if we do have a big land base."

In 2005, Emergency Services was added as a function, creating a challenge because there are many agencies involved. Janis says the CRD sometimes feels like a puppet in the middle, trying to define its role and help constituents when they are facing floods, fires, or other emergencies. Sometimes senior government agencies swoop in and call the shots, and the conflicting roles can frustrate residents and agencies alike.

"We do learn from every event, and the inter-agency coordination is gradually improving," Janice notes. "People who live in an area need to be part of the solution but they often feel left out, like they don't know anything. Ensuring their voice is heard through the many agencies involved is important to a successful outcome."

An ongoing challenge is educating people in the role of the regional district. "With a total budget of about forty million and a hospital district budget of another ten million, people really should know what the CRD is, and in particular what we're doing with their money," Janis points out. "Municipal representatives change fairly often, but rural directors are often elected by acclamation and they usually stay until they retire. This isn't necessarily a bad thing, but with no elections, constituents don't always know what the district's role is."

Janis believes an orientation package for candidates would be helpful so they would know what they are getting themselves into. "Sometimes new directors (and many constituents) don't realize there is no magic supply of money, you have to take money away from people to give it back to them."

CRD staff tends to stay. Many have tenure and have acquired expertise and experience in planning, research and building. Janis worries because some staff members are nearing retirement age and no one is coming up. People don't realize there are so many career opportunities in local government, and she would like to see local government on the school curriculum.

Working in local government has unique challenges. Balancing technical expertise and political discretion can be an art, Janis finds. "Trained technical staff can be frustrated when they come up with what they believe is the best technical solution to an issue, then the board does something else entirely. It drives them nuts, but they need to learn that staff is there to recommend, directors are there to make decisions."

She gives the board the best advice she can (whether they like it or not) and then accepts their decision "loyally, and, hopefully, enthusiastically" and implements their will regardless of whether or not they followed her recommendations. It would be easy for a CAO to direct the board, she says. When directors are new and don't know the rules, or are struggling to find a common vision, it would be easy for staff to take over, but, as she

Cariboo Regional District CAO Janis Bell has a busy work schedule but she always had time for her family, which now includes grandson Carter.

points out, "that is a dangerous trap to fall into. If staff is making the decisions, why bother with a board?"

The CRD belongs to a number of municipal organizations, so Janis does a fair amount of travelling. BC is the only province with a regional district level of government. "We learn from other provinces that have different systems," she says. "The CAOs compare notes and I always learn something." While she has learned a lot on the job, Janis has taken numerous courses on local government and completed her certificate in Public Administration at UNBC as well as earning her certificate in Local Government Administration from the BC Board of Examiners.

Janis sat on the other side of the governance table in the early 1990s as a Williams Lake city councillor. That came about after Reform Party members asked her to run for Member of Parliament. She had a three-year-old at home, and didn't know if she wanted to do that. She decided to try city council first.

"Between my work at the CRD and city council I was buried in paperwork," she says. "I didn't even have time to look at my own mail. At the beginning, other councillors were a bit suspicious of the CRD connection; they couldn't believe I could be neutral on some issues." After one term on council, she decided she didn't want to be an elected official.

One job she will never forget was the reorganization of the CRD's dozen volunteer fire departments. The district paid the expenses, but had no say in the operations. Local governments were facing increased liability for some services, and in 1988 Janis was given the task of making sure the fire departments were meeting appropriate standards. She expected some struggles, as fire departments were one of the last male dominions. As a twenty-eight-year-old blonde in high heels and a suit, she was not greeted warmly by the firemen.

"I fondly referred to the fire chiefs as the last of the dinosaurs," she recalls. "They were mostly older gentlemen and they were used to running their own shows. Firefighting is by necessity a military-style environment where chains of command and following orders are everything. I was not only the wrong gender, I knew nothing about firefighting."

She did, however, know about local government, liability, standards of care, and rules and regulations. Soon after she took the job, a delegation of North Cariboo firemen appeared before the board demanding her position be rescinded. They said they didn't need anyone from the CRD, let alone a woman, telling them what to do. The board held fast, but soon after, the South Cariboo fire departments invited her to a meeting. She says she should have been suspicious. "The meeting turned out to be a set-up to prove just how little I knew about firefighting, although by then I had learned quite a bit."

The fireman chosen to lead the charge came on full force, listing all her shortcomings. A gentleman sitting in the back of the room turned out to be a fire commissioner from Kamloops. "He'd heard about the planned coup. I'm not sure whether his role would have been to scrape up my remains at the end of the meeting or what, but I held my own, and likely surprised some people in the room," Janis says. The commissioner congratulated her not only on surviving the meeting, but winning the day.

"The fellow who led the charge that night turned out to be one of my favourite fire chiefs, one of my greatest supporters, and a personal friend. Those guys were all good-hearted community volunteers who liked things the way they were. Unfortunately, a lot of things needed to change, and slowly they did."

The position of manager of protective services was unique to the CRD and she was invited to other districts to explain the function. She says she became a huge fan of the volunteer firefighters and spent a lot of time developing policies to help them do their jobs, and fighting anything that hindered them. The policies were later applied in other parts of the province. "I learned things I never thought I'd know, like firefighting techniques, equipment, apparatus, understanding what a foot pound (or pound-foot depending on who you're talking to) of torque is."

After twelve years, Janis was asked to take on the additional role of acting administrator, and she again attended board meetings. That led to the position of deputy administrator, and two years later, to CAO.

Participating in the 2010 Olympic Games in Vancouver was one of her most rewarding experiences. The CRD led a consortium of local governments that banded together for BC Street. The 18,000 square-foot venue showcased the major regions of the province as part of the Olympic O Zone, a sixty-six-acre site organized by the City of Richmond. The Cariboo pavilion was based on the CRD's designation as Forest Capital of Canada for 2010 and 2011.

"We had 475,000 visitors over a sixteen-day period and the positive feedback was amazing. About 3.4 billion people either heard, read or saw a feature of BC Street worldwide. We partnered with non-profit agencies, private industry and different provincial ministries for a tremendous display of everything the Cariboo Chilcotin has to offer. It was done with volunteer effort by staff, elected officials, partners and folks like husbands who carted all the stuff we needed back and forth. Our goal was to bring the Cariboo to the world and the world to the Cariboo and we did just that," Janis says. The participation won the CRD numerous awards.

Every year Janis and her husband go to Mexico for two weeks to recharge their batteries, and they have a place at McLeese Lake where they go to relax. With six grown children between them, family keeps them busy. Janis unwinds and works off the day's stress at kickboxing and biking. She is one of five long-time friends, Columneetza classmates, who get together to go on trips and celebrate birthdays.

While there have been many career highlights, Janis believes her greatest lifetime accomplishment has been raising a "wonderful" daughter and now enjoying an "equally wonderful" grandson. "There are so many good things happening in our personal lives that we'd all need our own books to talk about them," she notes.

Cariboo Chilcotin School District

School District #27 (Cariboo Chilcotin) is geographically one of the largest in the province. Encompassing 88,000 square kilometres, it serves eighteen communities with 5,800 students in thirty schools. The schools range from small rural school to larger city schools. Because the area is so far flung, the district has a large bus fleet to get the students where they need to be.

The Board of Education, which consists of seven regionally elected trustees, is responsible for the district's operations in a co-governance model with the provincial government, which sets the curriculum and the budget.

As this is written, the district's top administrators are Diane Wright, CEO and Superintendent of Schools, and Bonnie Roller, Secretary Treasurer.

Diane Wright

Working With the Community

*D*iane Wright began her career in the Cariboo Chilcotin as a rookie schoolteacher. She retired thirty-five years later as the district's first female superintendent of schools.

Diane was born and raised in Vancouver. Her dad insisted she and her sister get an education that would end up in a job so they could be independent. At the time, jobs for women were usually teaching or nursing. The two took his advice, Diane becoming a teacher, her sister a nurse. When Diane finished the three-year teaching program at Simon Fraser University, she applied for schools north of Hope.

"I wanted adventure," she explains. She didn't think she'd find it in the Lower Mainland. When she was offered a job in Williams Lake, she found the town on the map, then accepted. The first year she taught a Grades 1/2 split at Poplar Glade School.

Many women teachers who came to the Cariboo married and stayed, and Diane was true to the tradition. She met Randy Wright, they married two years later, and moved to Alberta while Randy returned to school. Diane took a job on a national project that saw special needs children attend regular schools. When the Wrights returned to Williams Lake, Randy joined the local Ministry of Environment and

Diane went to Williams Lake Junior Secondary (WLJS), where she initiated the first class for special needs secondary school students in the district. This opened the door, and the next year saw thirty to forty students and another teacher in the program.

When their first daughter, Shalene, was born, Randy was doing contract work. It was off and on, and in between contracts he looked after the baby. Diane was at WLJS for six years, teaching some regular classes along with special education. Second daughter Tianna was born in 1984.

After WLJS, Diane went to the Skyline Alternate School. The program worked with teens who had experienced challenges and needed an alternative approach to school, and she says this was "a tremendous experience." After four years there, she went to Chilcotin Road Elementary. Randy was well established by then, and Diane took the opportunity to work part-time and finish her degree. An added bonus was that Shalene and Tianna attended the school and she could coach their sports teams. After dinner the three of them would sit down and the girls would do their homework while Diane prepared her lessons.

She went back to WLJS teaching outdoor education and working in the special education program for a year, and the next teaching opportunity came with a new off-site program the school district developed called CONNECT. It was a storefront classroom that operated on a drop-in basis in the downtown area. The intent was to

Diane Wright with her husband, Randy, and granddaughter, Scarlett. Diane retired in 2012 as School District #27's Superintendent of Education. She spent thirty-five years in the district, starting as a teacher. She counts the title "Nana" among her important accomplishments.

help vulnerable students progress academically while building life and social skills to meet personal goals. "This was where I learned the value of working with other agencies," Diane says. "It isn't possible for the school to do everything."

She liaised with community groups working with youth, such as the Child Development Centre, the Boys and Girls Club, Ministry of Children and Family Development and the RCMP along with individuals who were involved in different activities. The program served about seventy-five students a year who attended as they were able to. Some attended five days a week, others only once a week, but they all had a lifeline to the program, and staff was available in emergencies.

While she was working with CONNECT, Diane started Wright Gardens. This came about more or less by accident. Diane's work was demanding, and she needed to find a way to relax. "Getting her hands in the dirt" did that, as she has very green thumbs. She can grow everything and anything, and she did. She comes by her love and ability for growing things naturally. Her father was head groundsman for the Vancouver School District, and his father was a landscaper. On the maternal side, her grandmother was a member of the Vancouver Horticulture Society.

"It's in my genes," Diane says. When it got to the point where the house and yard were overrun with plants, Randy installed a greenhouse and they started in the nursery business. First they sold plants from the yard, then as the business grew, they sold to stores. The business was thriving, but then they ran out of a sufficient water supply to manage all the plants. They had to close the nursery, but Diane hasn't stopped growing plants.

After six years, CONNECT was the victim of district downsizing, and was absorbed by Skyline. Diane spent the next two years at Nenqayni, the residential wellness centre for First Nations families just outside Williams Lake. The school district provides the centre with a teacher and an aide for the family program. Diane and the aide taught students from kindergarten to Grade 12, all in one room. Beyond the academics, the progam was culturally based, and Diane says it was a wonderful learning experience for her as she became immersed in the First Nations culture, going to sweats, gathering sage, drumming and singing.

At times, though, she really felt like and outsider. "I talked too much, and didn't pause, and sometimes I said the wrong things," she says, "but everyone at the centre helped me with incredible courtesy and respect." An eagle feather, given to her by the parents of one of her students, has had a special place in her office.

A changeover in the district saw Diane in the post of vice-principal of student support services. The first year required part-time teaching vulnerable students, part-time administration work. The next year she was full-time district principal. She travelled all over the district working with teachers and support service staff to ensure the needs of students and all the ministry requirements were being met.

She visited every school, staying overnight in the more remote communities. The communities are diverse, and she was able to spend enough time in each one to get to know the families as well as the school staff.

"For programs to work, there must be a strong network and support services from the community," she explains. She found inspiration with the Community Planning Council of 100 Mile House. Because that community has fewer resources, everyone works closely together and collaborates, and it builds capacity.

Diane began working on her master's degree while she was at Nenqayni, and she finished it while at Support Services, graduating with a master of arts in Conflict Analysis and Management from Royal Roads.

In 2008 when the position of district superintendent came open, Diane applied and was appointed. Although she isn't the first local person to hold the position, she is the first woman and she is the first to be well known personally throughout the entire district. Diana was honoured at the 2011 International Women's Dinner, where Columneetza students paid tribute to her distinguished service to the district.

"I loved my work and enjoyed it," Diane says. "I have been fortunate to work with amazing teachers, principals, support staff, students and families." She adds, "Family is so important. I am looking forward to time with family and gardening, and my husband and I are making plans to travel."

And there is granddaughter, Scarlett, born in September 2010. "She has given me my most important accomplishment," Diane adds, "the title 'nana.'"

Bonnie Roller

Numbers Have Been a Big Part of Her Life

*B*onnie Roller is the first woman to hold the post of secretary treasurer for School District #27. The job is huge. The district is one of the Cariboo's major employers, with one thousand employees and an operating budget of over $55 million.

Bonnie was born and raised in Williams Lake. Her parents are long-time residents Doug and Floris Martineau. Bonnie was in Grade 10 at Williams Lake Junior Secondary school when the teacher in her typing class took on the task of placing students in Career Explorations, and he sent her to the school board office for her work week. For the next two years they called on her whenever they needed a relief receptionist.

She graduated from Columneetza in 1981, and just before the grad ceremony, an accountant from the district called her and said her computer had malfunctioned and she'd lost all her data, could Bonnie come and get it back for her. Bonnie did, and she stayed on working full-time in the accounting department. Over the years she's held every role from training in reception through all finance positions including payroll, to her present position. Working with numbers has been a big part of her life.

"I changed jobs every four or five years," she explains. She started working on her CGA in 1991, and received her degree in 2005. Fred Harkies was the secretary treasurer when she began with the district, and she worked under Andy Sullivan, Don Woytowich and Leo Bacon. When the job became vacant, the school board offered her the position without posting it. "That was a high spot," she says.

Along with minding the store in the finance department, Bonnie's job calls for attending many meetings and writing many reports. "As strange as it may seem, I really enjoy writing reports," Bonnie says with a smile. In trustee election years, she is also the returning officer for the district.

Technology has made huge changes in the accounting department over the years. When Bonnie began there was a manual system, and while there are still a few manual tasks (an occasional cheque needs to be made out) most of the accounts are on computer. The payroll is done electronically. The speed is great, Bonnie says, but the downside is that a number of jobs have been lost because of the technology.

Assisting the board in setting the annual budget is a great challenge. Funding is a perennial problem; the province funds school districts on a per-pupil basis. Province-wide, most districts have declining enrollment. "I encourage conservative budgeting with the economic and resource challenges in our district," Bonnie explains. "The student population has been dropping by about 150 students a year. In our heyday we had about 9,500 students. Today we have about 5,500, and the fewer students, the fewer dollars from the province, but the costs of operating the system don't go down proportionately."

That sounds depressing but Bonnie says the upside is seeing what has been accomplished in terms of the achievement levels of district students in spite of the financial restrictions.

"We are all here to work together as a team for the best education of the students," she says.

Bonnie and Superintendent Diane Wright have been together in administration for some years and they work well together. Diane has put together an excellent management team and Bonnie credits everyone on the district staff for working together.

"It makes a marked difference in the results," she says. "And we have shown constant improvement in most educational areas over the past few years."

Secretary Treasurer Bonnie Roller, left, was born and raised in Williams Lake. Her career with School District #27 began with a high school career week and she worked her way up the ladder to one of the two top posts. She is pictured here with her sisters, Diane Martineau of West Kelowna and Bev Sheldon of Vernon.

Bonnie started her own education in District #27 at the Puss n' Boots Kindergarten in 1967. It was located where the new firehall is now. She went to Marie Sharpe Elementary, starting in 1968, and remembers the ceremony when the name of the school was changed from Williams Lake Elementary to Marie Sharpe, in honour of the long-time elementary school teacher. Bonnie then attended Williams Lake Junior Secondary and graduated from Columneetza Senior Secondary.

In 1982 she married Perry Roller, a heavy-duty mechanic at Gibraltar Mines and they had one son, Clayton. Sadly, Perry died of cancer in 2001, leaving Bonnie as the single mother of a teenager. She says it was the most difficult time of her life.

"I was used to my husband being the disciplinarian, and it was difficult for me to do that as well as going through the grieving process," she says, "but we survived, and Clayton is a wonderful young man." Clayton currently lives in Williams Lake with his wife, Jana, and their new child, Asher Perry Nolan Roller, who was born in June 2012.

Bonnie remarried and with her husband, Dan Routley, owns and operates two movie stores, Movies on the Go in Williams Lake, and Valley Video at 150 Mile. The latter store also has the post office and Sears catalogue outlet. Bonnie does the books for both businesses. They also share raising Dan's son, Jordon, who goes to Columneetza. Jordon sometimes forgets Bonnie isn't his birth mother. "I take this as the ultimate compliment and tell him to always remember that I chose him and that he is very special to me," she says.

Bonnie's job is not always nine to five. School district events, especially meetings, are held when it's convenient for the attendees, be they trustees or members of the public, so it isn't easy to balance work with the family. Dan and Jordan are great about sharing household duties, she says. "I couldn't do it without them."

Bonnie doesn't have much spare time. She has allergies (she says she's allergic "to everything"), which limits her outdoors activities, but she does a lot of reading, and watches a lot of movies, which is part of being in the movie business.

The school district has been a large part of her life, and she enjoys her professional work and personal relationships with her colleagues. "I have been blessed and very lucky in my life, and wouldn't change a thing. Even during the hardest times, the people I work with were pillars of support and I love every minute of it."

Helen Haig-Brown

Her Heart Is in the Chilcotin

Award-winning filmmaker Helen Haig-Brown found no joy in school when she was younger, particularly high school. She was always very much into sports, especially hockey and soccer, and music, but she says she was never focused enough on any one thing "to get phenomenally good at doing it."

"I had no self-esteem, no will power, and school was monotonous," she says. At nineteen she was still trying to graduate. Her dad realized her heart wasn't in it and told her if she gave up on school he'd buy her a ticket to cross "any ocean she wanted to."

"I thought this was crazy," she says. "When I told him I still wanted to graduate he told me I was kicked out—he wanted to force me to move on."

She responded by moving out and getting her own place so she could try to finish high school, but that didn't last long. She did quit school, and went to Whistler where she worked as a snowshoe guide and saved for her travels. She spent a year travelling in Australia and South Asia, then came home and registered as a mature student at Langara College.

Helen Haig-Brown works in all kinds of places and under all kinds of circumstances, and she isn't deterred by a bit of snow. An award-winning cinematographer, Helen was raised in two cultures, Anglo-Canadian from her dad, Tsilhqot'in from her mother.

One of her first assignments was to make a presentation, either oral, in writing, or video. She chose video but didn't know where to begin. Her teacher suggested recording something from TV, but Helen decided to film something herself. She borrowed her brother's Hi8 camera and once she got started, she became so involved she couldn't focus on anything else.

She had access to the school equipment room for an hour a day for editing, but she didn't know how to use the equipment and there wasn't time to learn. She solved that problem by jamming the equipment room door so it wouldn't lock, and she sneaked in and camped over the weekend. A friend helped her edit her film.

She was hooked. She realized film was a way to tell the stories, traditional, historic and contemporary, about the conflicts, pain, suffering and triumphs in the First Nations communities. "I wanted to record people telling the stories that needed to be talked about and shared within the Native community," she says. "I'd never been so happy before but I knew I had to develop the skills to do the stories justice."

There are storytellers on both sides of Helen's family. Her paternal grandfather, Roderick Haig-Brown, was a noted Canadian author. Her dad, Alan, taught school in the Cariboo Chilcotin then changed gears when the family moved to Vancouver. He is now an internationally known writer. Her mother, Maria, is a member of the Myers family of Stone (Yunesit'in) in the Chilcotin country. Her family knows and tells the traditional Tsilhqot'in stories and songs, and what's more, they have recorded them.

Helen spent her early years at Stone. She attended school at Alexis Creek (she remembers spending what seemed like forever on the bus). She was seven when the family moved to Vancouver where her mother attended UBC. They came home for holidays. When her parents separated, her dad stayed on the coast and her mother returned to Stone. Helen and her sister, Linda, spent the next ten years going back and forth between two different places, two different cultures: a strong Anglo-Canadian academic background and a traditional Tsilhqot'in.

"We were split between the two. In a lot of ways it was conflictive, it was difficult to stay balanced," she says, adding with a grin, "I seem to have spent my whole life changing gears."

Once she decided on a filmmaking career, Helen dropped out of Langara and set about getting the skills she needed. She didn't care for academics, so a four-year program was out. She didn't want to be told how to tell stories, either, she just wanted the technical skills to get them on film. She took a week-long intensive media training program, followed by a four-month program for aboriginal youth through the Indigenous Media Arts Group. Capilano College's Indigenous Independent Digital Filmmaking program came next and that's where she discovered the artistic side of filmmaking. She began experimenting with different styles and she hasn't looked back. As a cinematographer she has worked with leaders in the field of experimental films on CBC, the Knowledge Network and the National Film Board.

Helen's most recent film, *Legacy*, is an autobiographical documentary. It shares the stories of five generations of women in her family's struggle with the different forms of colonization, and how the struggle has shaped ideas of intimacy, bonding, love and healthy relationships within her family and within herself.

Her film *Su Naa* (My Big Brother) won Best Experimental Film at the imagineNATIVE 2005 Film and Media Arts Festival. She was the cinematographer for *Writing the Land* and *Nikamowin,* which screened at the 2008 Sundance Film Festival. She collaborated with her aunt, York University professor Celia Haig-Brown, on the documentary film *Pelq'ilc* (Coming Home) which tells how the descendants of the former Kamloops Indian Residential School students are regenerating the Secwepemc culture and language. As she progressed, Helen says she became less rule-oriented.

"My mother and sister and aunts and uncles are the knowledge keepers..."

In 2009 she was invited to the Embargo Collective, an initiative the imagineNATIVE Film Festival held to celebrate its ten-year anniversary. She was one of seven indigenous artists from around the world who were put together to talk about their creative process. Helen was challenged to do a science-fiction video in a language other than English, something she had never done before. She rose to the occasion by telling a traditional Tsilhqot'in story in the Tsilhqot'in language. *The Cave* is the tale of a hunter who rode his horse into a cave and was transported to another world. Named one of the top ten films by the 2009 Toronto International Film Festival Group, it was an official selection at the Berlinale 2010 Film Festival, and was selected to screen in competition at the 2011 Sundance festival.

Helen says Sundance is the best festival of all. "I tend to get tired halfway through most festivals but not there. I found Berlin cold, but Sundance is in a small village and it's well hosted."

There have been difficult moments along the way. She was invited to participate in a film festival in New York, and, caught up in the excitement of having "made it" to the big time, she treated herself to an expensive pair of boots with high heels. She wasn't used to high heels and they made her feet hurt. "When the boots hurt my feet, I wondered if this idea of success might also be hurting my spirit, or my natural self," she says. "I wondered what I was doing there."

Helen's heart has always been in the Chilcotin, but before she could go home to stay, she had to make a name for herself, and that meant living in the big cities. She has paid her dues now, and since 2009 the Chilcotin has been her home base.

"I travel most of the time, flying out to jobs in Yellowknife or Santa Fe, wherever, but the Chilcotin is my home," she says. "When you come back, you see through a new lens, you see the beauty in the land, in the people, in the culture. You see it and feel it when you reach the top of Sheep Creek. When I was younger I only saw the poverty and the drinking and no jobs, and I thought there were no options, just pain."

One of her conflicts has been balancing the light side with the more serious, between making films that are fun and ones that are important, but she says it is getting easier to go into the lighter side. She collaborates with both sides of her family. Her mother and sister and aunts and uncles are the "knowledge keepers," she says. "I've always been following them or have been taught by them in some way."

The Myers family has a collection of video and audio recordings from the 1970s. Helen's great-uncle was the inspiration for *The Cave*, and her current project, *The Legacy*, is a feature documentary telling the story of five generations of the women in her family. She's using family archives, stories, songs and footage to tell of the incredible women who went through 150 years of hardships, from smallpox and the Tsilhqot'in war to residential schools. She believes the women's sense of loneliness, grief, and trauma started long before residential schools. She wants to face the issues but she also wants to celebrate the women's survival. "It's the story of strong, incredible, resilient women and their power to survive," she says.

Helen's long-term goal is to have a residential arts centre in the Chilcotin, preferably by the river (she has a spot in mind), where artists and people from around the world could come to train and develop local talent. Helen says there are many gifted young people who are potential actors, filmmakers, and artists. "It really is important for the younger people to see the beauty of where they come from, for them to express their feelings. It's a way of healing."

Along with filmmaking Helen sits on a number of boards, and she conducts media training for youth. She says for years people at home didn't know what she was doing. Even her mom would say, "Oh, she does films or something."

Now they know.

Rosanna McGregor

Cariboo Friendship Centre

*T*he Cariboo Friendship Society has been serving urban aboriginals in Williams Lake since 1967. Executive Director Rosanna McGregor has been with the organization for twenty-two of those years.

In 1990 Rosanna was working for realtor Glen Woods at ReMax, and she often had lunch at the Cariboo Friendship Centre (CFC), which was just next door. She was well aware of the centre's activities as her late aunt, Bonnie Keener, and her uncle, George Keener, were founding members of the centre, and George is the long-time chair of the society. When Executive Director Gail Madrigga offered her a job in the accounting department, Rosanna was interested. She enjoyed working for ReMax, but she wasn't keen on making a career in real estate.

"I don't think I could be a salesperson," she says, so she went to work for the centre in accounts payable. She worked her way up the administrative ladder, taking on responsibility for tenant relations and social programs. She became assistant director in 2003 and director in 2011. She follows a CFC tradition—almost all the executive directors have been women.

Rosanna's parents, Molly Thomas and Dave Felker, lived at the Hamilton Ranch in Beaver Valley, and Rosanna grew up with horses and farm animals. Her dad, who was a faller in the lumber industry, guided with Pete and Tommy Hamilton in the autumn and there were "tons of hunters" on the ranch. The nearest neighbour was four kilometres away and Rosanna rode either her bike or her horse to visit friends. She went to Big Lake Elementary School. Both her parents went to St. Joseph's Mission, her dad only until Grade 5, when he had to go to work on the family ranch at Felker Lake. Her mother, a member of the Williams Lake Band, was a student until Grade 9. Rosanna says her only knowledge of being Indian came from visits to her grandmother at Sugar Cane.

"When my mother got mad at Dad she'd go home to Sugar Cane, but I stayed with him," she recalls. "I thought everyone there was either a drunk or a street person."

When her grandmother, Rosie William, died in 1983, Rosanna and her mother spent some time at Sugar Cane and Rosanna had her first experience with Secwepemc traditions. "There were so many things I knew nothing about, like washing the walls with juniper after a death, the prayers, food, tobacco, gambling. Most important was learning that I belonged to a community of proud First Nations."

Rosanna attended Williams Lake Junior Secondary and, after graduating from Columneetza, went to Fraser Valley College (now the University of the Fraser Valley). She raised money for her education by breaking and training two

Rosanna McGregor, the executive director of the Cariboo Friendship Centre, was raised on a Cariboo Ranch. In the picture she is in the egg basket being carried by her mother, Molly Thomas.

horses, which she then sold. Her paternal grandmother Ruth Felker, who had a big influence in her life, matched whatever money Rosanna saved for her education.

"I knew there would be serious consequences from her if I didn't go to college," Rosanna says.

Both Dave and Molly were chronic alcoholics. Molly, who worked at the stock-yards, had been a weekend drinker, but then began drinking more. "The older I got the more she drank and the more I dreaded weekends," Rosanna recalls. In the 1970s, Molly's sister Bonnie Keener sobered up and went back to school to be a social worker. Rosanna begged her mother to stop but Molly couldn't do it.

"I learned to cherish the time she was sober," Rosanna says, adding, "I had to learn how to deal with alcoholism and to come to my own terms." Both her parents died relatively young, Molly at sixty-four, Dave at sixty-three.

"Never look down on anybody unless you are helping them up."

After college, Rosanna's first job was with the Williams Lake Band as education coordinator. She served briefly on the band council after winning a by-election. She was one of the "young ones" with Chief Alice Abbey, and she had the council's human resources portfolio. She did not enjoy elected office. She says she came out of school wearing rose-coloured glasses but soon learned life was different.

"Band members thought you had more power than you had. Some would get mad when they didn't qualify for post-secondary school, but I had to deal with facts. It took me years to mend fences," she says.

She left band-work in 1989 to work with Cariboo Indian Enterprises where she was involved in a "trap tree" project for Mountain Pine Beetles. She thinks it's possible that if this program had been adequately funded it might have prevented some of the later problems with the beetle infestations. Her next job was ReMax, and then the CFS.

As assistant director, Rosanna was asked to serve on many committees, including the Fetal Alcohol Spectrum Advisory Committee, which she sat on for eight years, Williams Lake Health Advisory, Social Planning, the Stampede Park Advisory (ten years), and the Aboriginal Housing Management Association since 1996. She's been on the Interior Health Board since 2006. As a member of the city's Social Planning Council, Rosanna had an interest in housing, and the need for social housing in the City of Williams Lake was identified. The Williams Lake Social Housing committee was formed with interested members of the Social Planning Advisory Network (SPAN) joining in and the result was Glendale Place, a thirty-four-unit affordable housing complex.

In 2007 the Friendship Society submitted a proposal to BC Housing for a thirty-three-unit apartment building in downtown Williams Lake. This was a major undertaking, and was three years in the works. The grand opening for the building, called the Eagle's Nest, was held in June 2010. The $8.2-million building is energy efficient, qualifying for the silver LEED (Leadership in Energy and Environmental Design).

Rosanna doesn't think lay people can get through this kind of building process without expert help. "There's just too much legalese," she says.

For a time it looked as though the house next door to the complex would have to be torn down to make room for parking for the building. The house had been the home of Rosanna's grandmother. "That hurt," she says. "I had so many memories of family gatherings there, but in the end it didn't have to go."

As executive director of the Friendship Centre, Rosanna oversees fifty-seven full-time and twenty-six part-time staff with a $2.8-million payroll. The centre offers a wide range of services to the whole community, not just the aboriginal community, from social services, recreation and cultural activities, education, economic development projects (restaurant, contracting, native arts, and craft shop) to social housing.

To function in today's competitive environment with its rules, regulations and legal and government compliances, Rosanna says you need a way of acquiring capital, marshalling technologies, implementing information systems, auditing performance, continuously improving quality, coordinating care and negotiating and dealing with public and private bureaucracies. She says the one frustrating thing about her work was, and is, that the bureaucratic rules keep changing. "You can guarantee that once you work your way through legislation, rules and contracts, they will be changed, and you have to tear everything up and learn the new ones."

Rosanna has a twenty-year-old daughter, Jaydeen, from her first marriage to Bill Sargent, from Canoe Creek. The marriage broke up in 1999. Rosanna is now married to Doug McGregor and they have a pre-teen daughter, Cambria. "One teenager down and one to go. I think they say something about payback," Rosanna says with a smile.

Rosanna and Doug, who is a floor layer, knew each other from years of playing fun ball. After she was single again they got to know each other better at the bowling alley where, she says, he flirted with her. The McGregors live at Sugar Cane and enjoy lots of camping, fishing, fun ball and gardening in the summer. They also enjoy any activity that includes friends and family, like snowmobiling, tobogganing or ice fishing to help pass the Cariboo winter.

Rosanna says the lesson she learned from her parents is to set up some healthy boundaries for herself and her daughters, and from her work, to "never look down on anybody unless you are helping them up."

Coleen Duggan

Nana Loves to Rodeo

Coleen Duggan, one of BC's better-known barrel racers, spent her early years on her parents' isolated ranch in the west Chilcotin.

In the early 1960s Coleen's dad, Dick Wright, realized his dream of having a ranch in the wilderness when he acquired the last homestead available in the Anahim Lake area in the west Chilcotin. By 1963 he had fences and a cabin built, and his wife, Maxine, and their four daughters came from Washington State to join him. Coleen, the third daughter, was seven years old.

That first cabin had a dirt floor. Pots and pans were hung from the rafters, and a tarpaulin on the roof kept out any leaks. Dick later put planks on the floor but the knots fell out and chair legs got stuck in the holes. Nailing tin can lids on the bottom of the chair legs solved that problem. They had no electricity, and the running water was provided by the people who ran to pack it.

The ranch wasn't really back of beyond, but access was difficult. Dick cut eight kilometres of the thirty-two-kilometre road to Anahim Lake by hand and it was seasonal (translation: impassible in some months). Snow blocked it in winter and in spring it was a quagmire. Their transportation was by saddle horse, team and wagon, or a tractor that started with a hand-crank. They got the mail every few months. CKWL message time was their other means of communication. People could send them messages via the Williams Lake radio station, but there was no way to get messages out. In an emergency, people could contact Baxter's Store at Anahim and someone would fly out to the ranch and drop a message—there was no landing spot for the plane.

The girls were the ranch crew. They helped hay in summer, feed the stock in the winter, and rode after livestock any time of year. When Dick was away working, they did everything. They were home-schooled by correspondence. Outside chores kept them busy during the day, and when the work was done, they'd sit at the kitchen table and do their lessons by the light of a Coleman lamp. Coleen finished Grade 8 by correspondence.

"People called us the gumboot cowgirls, we usually beat the boys."

The family's one outing was the yearly Anahim Lake Stampede. Coleen and sister Debbie entered every event they could, hoping to win the Junior All-Around Cowboy prize money.

"We didn't have riding boots, we wore spurs over gumboots. People called us the gumboot cowgirls," Coleen says, adding, "we usually beat the boys." They worked for a month on their entry for the stampede parade and usually won that too. The milk cow went to the stampede with them along with the team, saddle horses and dogs. "Once we cleared land for an arena so we could practise for stampede but it grew such good grass Dad wanted it for pasture," Coleen remembers.

Coleen had one very special horse, Laddie, that she got when she was eleven and he was two. She taught him all kinds of tricks. He died the year she was married, when he was eleven.

Coleen met Glenn Duggan at a stampede when they were both fifteen. Glenn was from Chezacut, another remote Chilcotin community. The next year they met again, and were impressed with each other, but the Wrights didn't make it to the next stampede (the only one they ever missed). Glenn kept in touch by writing to Coleen.

Dick and Maxine were taking cattle to the sale in Williams Lake that fall. There was a dance during the event and Coleen thought Glenn would be there. Maxine said Coleen and Debbie could join them if they could get a ride to town. It would be Coleen's first trip out farther than Anahim in eight years.

The girls managed to hitch a ride on a medical flight from Anahim, but they couldn't go in the ambulance to town, so they started walking. When they got to the highway, they didn't know which direction to go to get to Williams Lake, so they walked the two kilometres back up the hill to the airport where someone gave them

Coleen Duggan, one of BC's noted barrel racers, has been involved in rodeo for most of her life. When she isn't competing, she's training horses. She's had two special barrel racing horses, Sarge, and now Rainy Weather (pictured here).

a ride to town. They had the phone number to reach their parents but didn't know how to use the dial phone; Anahim had only crank phones. Just as a woman was helping them, they saw Maxine across the street.

They didn't have much in the way of clothes. They wore hand-me-downs and old boots. Debbie had been saving pennies—literally—and had twenty dollars in change. Coleen also had twenty dollars. They spent the money at Tony's Leather Store on shiny new cowboy boots. Maxine had made outfits for them to wear to the dance. Coleen's was a lavender-coloured vest and slacks.

After all that, Glenn didn't show up... and no one asked the girls to dance.

Glenn made up for his absence by riding to Anaham to see her later in the fall. It took him and his brother Terry twelve hours to ride the 120 kilometres of rough country from Chezacut to the Wright ranch. "For once in our lives, no one was home," Coleen says, "but they stayed until we did get home a few days later. When they left we had nothing to give them for their lunches except some corn bread and it fell apart. Glenn said it was the best lunch he ever had."

Not to be outdone, Coleen and Debbie returned the visit but it didn't turn out as planned. Coleen's lunch went astray, her horse lost a shoe, then they followed the wrong track. They ended up at Puntzi, sleeping under a tree. When they stopped at a place the next morning to ask directions, the man didn't even offer them coffee, he just pointed in the direction of Chezacut.

They arrived at Roy Mulvahill's ranch in Chezacut that afternoon. The Mulva-hills were astonished to see them so far from home on saddle horse. Debbie stayed there while Coleen rode to the Knoll ranch where Glenn's Aunt Mary gave her a fresh horse and directions to Duggans', seventeen kilometres farther in the bush. She arrived there to find Glenn and Terry were away looking for horses. The next day Glenn's mother, Hilda, gave her vague directions and a horse that knew its way home in case she got lost.

There was no real trail and she did get lost. Late in the afternoon she gave up and let the horse have its head, but instead of taking her back to Duggans', it took her to the brothers' camp. Glenn couldn't believe it when he saw her ride in. He took the sisters and their horses home by truck.

Dick had a sawmill business by then and was building houses in the Anahim area. When Glenn told him he wanted to marry Coleen, Dick said fine, but Glenn would have to work in the sawmill until they got to know each other. Glenn did that. It took awhile but he and Coleen were married at Anahim Lake.

At different times they lived at Anahim, Chezacut and Riske Creek. Along the way they had three children, Denise in 1978, Ray in 1979 and Stacey in 1983. Ray's arrival was both dramatic and traumatic. Coleen and Glenn were living way back in the bush beyond Chezacut where Glenn was logging. Coleen was seven months pregnant when the logging operation shut down, and on the way out on the bumpy road in a rickety truck, she went into labour. They stopped at Nimpo, where Sister Suzanne, the nursing nun from the Mission at Anahim Lake, was called in. Coleen was flown to Williams Lake Hospital where she spent two days lying flat on her back so she didn't lose the baby. Ray arrived weighing four and a half pounds.

They lived in Riske Creek for a few years where Glen had his own truck and hauled cattle. Their income was skimpy. For two years, four Duggans and two teen-age boarders lived on $150 a month. They did have a big garden. When things got better, Coleen wanted to go to veterinarian school in Alberta. Glenn was okay with that, but Dick invited him to go logging, so they returned to Anahim. The project had its ups and downs but when members of the Anahim Lake community part-nered with the Ulkatcho First Nations Band in a logging operation and mill, Glenn joined as a partner. This business was a success. The Duggans bought property near "downtown" Anahim, built a large house, and later, an indoor arena.

Wherever they were, Coleen and Glenn always had a few horses. At Anahim, the children rode in the BC Rodeo-sanctioned Chilcotin Rodeo circuit. Denise had her BC Amateur card but Coleen didn't start competing in barrel racing until later. "For one thing, I didn't have a good horse," she says. Glenn solved that by bring-ing a mare home when he made a trip to Vancouver. The mare bucked a lot at first, but Coleen got her going and won a number of events on her before giving her to Denise. Glenn then gave Coleen some money and sent her off horse-hunting. She and her sister went to Washington State and came back with two colts they bought off the racetrack. One was named Gastronomical. Coleen called him Sarge. She says he was a bad-ass and it took time to get him in line. "I'd spend hours riding him through a foot and a half of snow with my mom coming behind in case of trouble," she says.

She prevailed, and she would go on to win $50,000 with him before she sold him in 2011. They didn't always win though. At one rodeo when Sarge misbehaved, the winners got saddles, but all Coleen got was a T-shirt from her family saying, "Sarge, my job is to be difficult." Her current horse is called Rainy Weather.

Winter weather puts a stop to barrel racing in northern communities and Dug-gans' indoor arena solved that problem for a number of racers. Coleen held weekend competitions and barrel racers came from as far away as Houston and Prince George to participate. Glenn built an indoor swimming pool (the only one in the Chilcotin) and a hot tub, which added to the attraction. The sessions were family affairs with Maxine, Glen and Ray helping. Coleen used her profits to help pay for her events.

"We had some good times," she says. "We had fourteen regular riders, and it made a big difference to them being able to compete over the winter."

Once she started winning, Coleen decided to go professional but it isn't easy.

To qualify as a semi-professional, a contestant must win a thousand dollars in one rodeo season. Professional qualifications require winning a thousand dollars as a semi-pro in one season.

"You start at the bottom of seventy or more contestants," Coleen explains. She got her semi-pro permit in 2001, and her professional one in 2003.

The Duggans left Anahim Lake in 2004. The lumber business was doing well, but Glenn was ready for a change. He found it at Cache Creek, where he bought a machine shop. The move shaved two days off Coleen's travelling time to competitions, as it had previously taken a full day just to get to Williams Lake. She competes in about twenty pro rodeos a year in BC and Alberta, and makes the BC Rodeo Association finals most years. She's been in the top twenty in Canada a couple of times, was fourth in BC, and has qualified for Calgary three times. She's usually in the top ten of the pro rodeos she competes in. Not bad for a grandmother.

Along with barrel racing, Coleen trains and sells horses. At any one time she might be working with four horses at their acreage just outside of Cache Creek. She is known for her excellent horses.

Barrel racing isn't for the faint-hearted, and neither is training horses. Coleen has had her share of bumps, bruises, and being bucked off into prickly pear cacti. She sometimes shoes her own horses (few women do) and occasionally "tacks one on" for fellow barrel racers when needed at an event.

Coleen grows a large garden in the summer, and is a talented musician. She plays the guitar and sings, and she writes songs for rodeos and special occasions like weddings. In the winter she does a lot of sewing. Her specialty is making western-style clothes for her nine grandchildren; shirts for the boys, dresses for the girls. And the grandchildren all know that Nana loves to rodeo.

Chief Marilyn Baptiste

Her Goal Is to Keep the Land and Culture Intact

Marilyn Baptiste was born a few months before her father Marvin was elected chief of the Nemiah Band. He led the small Tsilhqot'in Band, now known as Xeni Gwet'in in First Nations Government, for ten years. Marilyn grew up being very aware of what was going on in the community and in politics. "From a young age I could see that one day I would be chief," she says. "I wanted to follow in Dad's footsteps." And she did. She was elected chief in February 2008.

The Nemiah Valley nestles in the mountains, some 120 kilometres from the Chilcotin Highway, 235 kilometres from Williams Lake. There wasn't a proper road into the valley until 1973 when the Canadian Army built a bridge across the Taseko River, and because of its inaccessibility, the land is much as it has ever been. The valley is breathtakingly beautiful, surrounded by snowcapped mountains, Chilko Lake and numerous crystal clear creeks and streams. There is an abundance of wildlife and vegetation. The people of Xeni Gwet'in live close to the land and rely on the natural resources. As chief, Marilyn's goal is to keep both the land and the culture intact for future generations.

"It's an inherited duty and responsibility," she says.

Marjorie Schuk, at Farwell Canyon in the Chilcotin country, has been involved with two generations of First Nation politics. Her husband, Marvin, was chief of the Xeni Gwet'in Band, and now, some years later, her daughter Marilyn holds the position.

Marilyn's mother, Marjorie, is the daughter of pioneers Joe and Katie Schuk. Joe went to the Chilcotin during the Depression and settled in the Tatlayoko Valley to ranch. Katie is the daughter of Tatlayoko pioneer ranchers Harry and Emelia McGhee. Tatlayoko is on the other side of the mountain from Nemiah and is an equally beautiful spot; it's part of the Xeni Gwet'in Caretaker territory.

Marvin, a member of the Nemiah nation, was a rancher and game guide. The Baptistes were living off-reserve at Chilanko Forks when then chief Sammy William asked Marvin to run for chief, and the family moved to Nemiah.

Marilyn and her three sisters grew up there. Their nearest neighbour was a half kilometre away. The Baptistes had horses and the girls learned to handle livestock, to dip net for fish, and to live in harmony with the land. Marilyn went to the Nemiah elementary school, then to Kamloops, Williams Lake and Chilliwack for secondary school. As a teenager, she was employed at Student Challenge jobs in the valley, working in the fields and taking care of elders. After the birth of her son Rickey she went to stay with her cousin in Alberta, and for a time she was on welfare. "That was horrible, I hated it," she says.

She went back to Nemiah as band manager trainee, a year-long position, but the band manager left in six months, telling her she was "good to go" with the job. She wasn't, so she went to work for her dad's logging company. During that time she acquired her first car through a first buyers' program to build credit on her own. That gave her a good start.

She later spent some time in Williams Lake working with her mother on janitorial jobs, and she enjoyed that. It was the right work for her at the time. "I liked working on my own and I liked the physical work," she says.

When she was ready for a change, Marilyn applied everywhere for a job, but she didn't get any interviews. She says she couldn't even get a job as a chambermaid. She finally connected with the Nenqay Law Centre. It was first located at the Anaham

Reserve (Tl'etinqox) then relocated to Williams Lake. She was hired as a secretary with the legal staff and held the job for nine years. She said it was a wonderful experience, but as so often happens, the centre closed when government funding was cut. Marilyn says it was devastating to see the centre close, as it had served the people well.

While she was at the centre and later, Marilyn travelled with Rickey, who was playing hockey in the Williams Lake minor hockey league with his Native team, the Cariboo Young'uns (Jr. Coyotes) and attending hockey school.

When her sister Sharon went on maternity leave, Marilyn went to Nemiah to fill in at Naghtaneged, the Nemiah elementary school, as a teacher's aide, library aide and noon supervisor. Her next job was with the Carrier Chilcotin Tribal Council (CCTC), in Williams Lake. It began as temporary but turned out to be long-term. While she was there she took a course with Lana Squinas, the CCTC's family support worker. It included lessons in public speaking with Bert Groenenberg and Toastmasters. That training proved to be valuable when she became chief. Marilyn speaks very quietly and effectively, without ever raising her voice.

Marvin passed away in 2003 and this was a difficult time for Marilyn because he had always been there for her. She and her dad had talked about her running for chief, but one issue held her back. Like many of her generation, she doesn't speak the Tsilhqot'in language. "I know what it's like to be on the outside, not understanding what's being said," she says.

It took time for Marilyn to get back to the Xeni Gwet'in community, but the opportunity came when she applied for and was accepted as sssistant project coordinator for the band's Cultural Tourism program. She found herself doing several jobs.

"There was so much that needed to be done and we didn't have the resources or the time to do everything," she says. "Sometimes people were doing five jobs at once."

The only way she got any balance in her life was to go on long walks. She likes to go up the mountains but seldom has time to do that now.

Some band members didn't see her lack of speaking the Tsilhqot'in language as a problem and lobbied her to run for chief. When she made up her mind to do it, she didn't tell anyone, including her boss at Cultural Tourism, until the last minute, but she did put it in the newsletter prior to the election. She won over the incumbent, Roger William. Roger knows the political ropes in dealing with government agencies, and he stayed on as a councillor and advisor.

Marilyn hit the ground running. Her first challenge was a Cariboo Indian Enterprises Ltd. meeting at Anaham Reserve. She knew something about the process from her dad, but even so it was a bit intimidating. The First Nations Mining Summit in Prince George in October 2008 was a milestone for her. One of the outcomes

Amnesty International held a meeting in Williams Lake in December 2011, to discuss the rights of indigenous people, and how this relates to the development of the Prosperity Mine in Tsilhqot'in territory. The topic was a weighty one, but Chief Marilyn Baptiste and her predecessor, former chief Roger William, shared a laugh during a break in the proceedings. Photo: Krista Liebe.

of that meeting was the formation of the First Nations Women's Advocating Responsible Mining. Chief Bev Sellars of the Xat'sull Band (Soda Creek) chairs this group.

The Xeni Gwet'in have always punched above their weight. During the Cariboo gold rush in the early 1860s, what is known as the Chilcotin War started in their back yard. The "war" stopped miners from building a road through their territory. In the 1990s the band stopped logging in their territory. When Marilyn took over as chief, Nemiah was already in the news because of a landmark court case over land rights. In 2002, the band went to court with the William Case, on behalf of the Tsilhqot'in, claiming title to traditional territory. It is a complicated matter, and it was five years before Supreme Court Justice David Vickers ruled, in a precedent-setting decision, that the band has rights to hunt and trade in the area, and he indicated there was an argument for recognition of title. The BC provincial, federal and Xeni Gwet'in governments all appealed on different aspects of the ruling.

A proposal from Taseko Mines Ltd. for a massive copper/gold mine to be located in the Xeni Gwet'in area catapulted Chief Marilyn into both provincial and national headlines.

Prospectors had been seeking gold in the area for years. When Taseko Mines Ltd. joined the search, federal regulations prohibited the destruction of fish-bearing waterways. This made mining in the Fish Lake area out of reach economically, but when the government changed the regulations, Taseko proceeded with plans for a mine they called Prosperity. The provincial and local governments and local businesses supported the plan. The Tsilhqot'in National Government (TNG) and neighbouring Secwepemc bands, with support from the Carrier, as well as numerous environmental groups, opposed it. A panel appointed by the Canadian Environmental Assessment Agency (CEAA) spent the better part of a year hearing the pros and cons of the proposal. Chief Marilyn and TNG chair Chief Joe Alphonse were the main spokespersons in the ensuing war of words.

In November 2010 the CEAA panel found the potential negative environmental impacts of the mine outweighed the economic benefits and the federal government rejected the proposal. It was one of only three ever turned down. The opponents of Prosperity breathed a sigh of relief but the victory was short-lived. A few months later the federal government gave the CEAA approval to consider another proposal from Taseko. As this is written that process is ongoing.

The 2010 four-day Run for Sacred Water called attention to the need for all humanity to protect pristine water sources. Sacred water from sources in Xeni Gwet'in, carried in four hand-held vessels, was relayed from the shores of Teztan Biny (Fish Lake) to the Williams Lake stampede grounds, arriving just before the stampede began. Participants could run, walk or ride. Chief Marilyn Baptiste was among the drummers. Photo: Krista Liebe.

The federal process focused on the environmental impacts of the proposed mine, but Marilyn is just as concerned over the cultural and considerable social impacts on the people.

Drumming has always played a big part of First Nations' culture, and Marilyn makes sure the spiritual side is acknowledged by insisting every gathering is opened with drumming. During the CEAA's hearings in Williams Lake, the secretariat accompanying the panel asked her not to drum inside the meeting room after the first day of the hearings, so she took the drummers outside.

She won the first battle in the second round, facing down machines and workers (accompanied by RCMP officers) who had a permit from the province to do exploratory work in the area before the federal process began. The court issued a temporary injunction to keep them out. At issue is the provincial government's legal obligation to adequately consult with the First Nations on resource proposals, and a compromise was reached. The injunction was later lifted with the Xeni Gwet'in consent.

The mine proposal is at the forefront, but it isn't the only item on Marilyn's agenda. In June 2012 the BC Court of Appeal came down with its decision on the William Case, affirming aboriginal rights but dismissing title except for site-specific claims. The TNG plans to take the issue of land title to the Supreme Court of Canada.

The Xeni Gwet'in have many activities in the works. On the economic side, they have tourism, logging, ranching, gardens and trapping. The band runs many of its own social activities including the elementary school, health services and a seniors' department. As chief, Marilyn does a lot of travelling to meetings both in and outside the province.

In December 2010 the First Nations Women's Advocating Responsible Mining received the Environmental Award from the Canadian Boreal Initiative for its work. Chief Marilyn was acclaimed secretary treasurer of the BC Union of Indian Chiefs, and she holds the same position with the Tsilhqot'in National Government. In 2011 she received the prestigious Eugene Environmental Award from the Wilderness Committee for her work on behalf of the Tsilhqot'in Nation to protect Fish Lake and the surrounding environment from the Prosperity Mine. The Wilderness Committee is Canada's largest member-based, citizen-funded wilderness preservation organization.

In the meantime, Marilyn says, "We keep talking, but no one in government or industry seems to be listening. All we can do is build on our victories."

Marilyn's mother, Marjorie, who had the distinction of being the wife of a chief and now the mother of a chief, lives in Williams Lake and is employed at the Cariboo Friendship Centre. She says one thing hasn't changed in the four decades since her husband was chief. "Marvin spent much of his time hassling with the federal government trying to resolve issues, and Marilyn does the same."

Joan Palmantier Gentles

She Walks the Talk

*J*oan Palmantier Gentles is not one to sing in the complaint chorus. She picks up the baton and leads the way. She has spent her adult life working to ensure First Nations people receive equality and justice, and that they preserve their culture while integrating into the mainstream society. She is quick to point out that no one achieves anything alone, that it takes teamwork, but she has been a catalyst for change as a BC Tel employee, courtworker, counsellor, educator, mentor and rodeo star.

Joan's dad was rodeo legend Leonard Palmantier, a founder of the Williams Lake Stampede, and once BC's All Around Cowboy. Her mother, Josephine Grambush, was a member of the Toosey Band (Tlesqox). Along with her own family, Josephine raised numerous grandchildren, nieces and nephews in times of need, as well as some other youngsters who came along.

Joan was born and raised at Riske Creek. She learned ranching and rodeo skills from her dad, bothers and neighbours. She learned the Tsilhqot'in language and culture from her mother and her mother's family. The Palmantiers worked together haying, riding with cattle, ranching, trapping, hunting, fishing and whatever else was required. Horses played a huge role in their lifestyle. The children rode from an early age with the Chilcotin plateau as their playground. Leonard never owned a vehicle; horse-drawn wagons and sleighs and saddle horses were their transportation.

Joan Gentles began her public career in 1966 as the Williams Lake Stampede Queen. She went on to become BC Indian Princess, and in 1967, Centennial Year, she was chosen to be Canadian Indian Princess.

When Joan did travel by vehicle, she tended to get sick going up or down the steep, windy Sheep Creek Hill.

Joan and her brothers became rodeo stars, as did some of their children. Leonard was inducted into the BC Cowboy Hall of Fame in 2000. The next generation of Palmantiers, including Joan, was inducted in 2006.

Joan began competing at local gymkhanas when she was ten. Her brother Jack built a chute and arena out of sight of the Palmantiers' house, where he practised bronc riding. Joan was both gate-opener and pickup man. When she started rodeoing, she had no way of transporting her horse, so she borrowed horses from other competi-

Joan began rodeoing when she was ten years old. She often competed in what were considered men's events such as steer riding and the Pony Express Race.

tors. She competed in barrel racing, steer undecorating, goat tying, breakaway roping, heading and heeling in team roping, mounting and hazing for steer wrestlers, mounting and hazing for the ladies steer undecorators, and mounting team ropers. The Pony Express Race was considered a man's sport but Joan won every race she entered. In those days they rode three horses and used one saddle. The contestant had to unsaddle and saddle each horse. She did some bush track racing on her competition horses. Along the way she encouraged many young competitors, lending her horse to give them the chance to compete on a seasoned mount. Along with bringing home her share of the winnings, Joan was known as the sharpest dresser on the circuit. She was particularly known for her hats; she was rarely seen without one.

Joan went to Riske Creek Elementary school, then Williams Lake Junior Secondary. In the fall of 1962, when she was sixteen, Joan's world turned upside down when her father and younger sister died within weeks of each other. She stayed home for a time to help her mother and took her schooling by correspondence. She finished high school in Williams Lake then she was off to business college in Kamloops.

Encouraged by Rita Place, the 1933 Stampede Queen, Joan ran for and won the 1966 Williams Lake Stampede Queen contest. Rita's husband, Hilary, was a Chamber of Commerce member and the group sponsored Joan. She spent a good deal of time the next year representing Williams Lake at events throughout the province.

There was a certain amount of racism in the community back then, sometimes subtle, sometimes overt, and because of it, some First Nations women, especially younger women, were reluctant to acknowledge their heritage. Not Joan. She entered the queen contest wearing a buckskin outfit she had made herself, proudly claiming her First Nations status. Looking back, she says the stampede queen experience gave her confidence.

"No one was expecting a squaw to speak out,"she says with a wry smile. Her take on racism is succinct. She says it's like saying a white horse is better than a black one. Her reaction to racism is direct. If anyone makes a disparaging remark about anything relating to First Nations people in her presence, she responds forcibly, no matter who makes the statement.

She was asked to compete in the Miss Cariboo contest, but she wasn't keen on parading around in a bathing suit (she said her brothers always teased her about being bowlegged), and when the Williams Lake Indian Band's Homemaker Club asked her to represent them at the BC Indian Princess Pageant in Vancouver on the same date, she saw this as an out. She won that title, making her eligible for the Canadian Indian Princess Pageant in 1967 (Canada's centennial year) in Winnipeg. She says she felt out of her league in that contest, but she won. She was crowned and wore the banner of Indian Princess at Expo 67. The win brought recognition not only to her, but to BC, the Williams Lake Indian Band, Williams Lake and her family. She was given the royal treatment when she returned from Expo 67 first in Vancouver, then in Williams Lake.

Described in the media as a "green-eyed, brunette beauty," Joan led a busy life as Canadian Indian Princess, attending all kinds of functions, including the Calgary Stampede, and always carrying the flag for Williams Lake and First Nations. Her personal projects for the year included supporting and promoting the building of the local Friendship Centre, and encouraging First Nations people to be proud of their heritage, speaking their languages, and practising their culture.

When her royal duties were over Joan went to work for the BC Telephone Company, first as a toll operator, then as a supervisor and trainer. She was there for seven years. She married Bill Gentles, also a keen rodeo competitor, and continued to follow the BC rodeo circuit. Their son Wade followed their footsteps, entering events as soon as he was old enough.

Because Joan speaks both the Tsilhqot'in and Secwepemc languages, she was often called to interpret in court, and she assisted many First Nations people through the justice system. Aware of this volunteer work, Provincial Court Judge Cunliffe Barnett encouraged her to apply for the Native Courtworkers' posting. She did, and spent three and a half years on this job. When she left she served on the provincial board for the BC Native Courtworkers Association.

Joan was instrumental in making changes in the justice system, and she is still a strong advocate for improvements, but the courtwork convinced her that if changes were going to come about for First Nations people, they would come

For health reasons, Joan can no longer compete in the rodeo arena. Recently she has turned her talents to dancing and now competes at powwows across the province.

through education. With that in mind she went back to school in 1976. She received her bachelor of education with honours from the University of British Columbia in 1980. Her first teaching position was at Mountview Elementary School, near Williams Lake. The Mountview principal was pleased to report that "Mrs. Gentles had made an excellent beginning to what will become a distinguished career." Prophetic words.

In 1983 she was seconded by UBC to become the Native Indian Teacher Education Program (NITEP) Field Coordinator in Williams Lake, teaching and coordinating first-and second-year university students' activities. NITEP asked her to go to Victoria to do the program there, but she went back to teaching in Williams Lake. "It's pretty hard to rodeo from Victoria," she explained.

"...the Creator does not send more hardships than a person can bear."

She later became Native education co-ordinator for Cariboo Chilcotin School District #27, and in 1994 she was named director of instruction for the First Nations Department. Along with her work in the schools, Joan held workshops for parents on a wide variety of issues ranging from the impact of residential schools and colonization to coordinated building self-esteem and healing activities. At one point she mortgaged her home to assist people to participate in personal and healing seminars. The participants assisted in fundraising to repay the mortgage. She has participated on many committees and boards at the local, provincial, and federal levels, and she found time to earn her master's degree in counselling from the University of Victoria.

Along with competing and helping youth along the rodeo road, Joan started field-judging rodeo events. While sitting a season out with a broken leg, she became the first certified female judge in BC and the first to get 100 percent on the written exam. She later assisted with judging seminars. At home, she raised horses and Corriente cattle for pleasure and personal use. She also had some bucking bulls for Wade to practise on. She contracted and sold stock to contractors and team ropers, and she leased bulls to ranchers for their first calvers. Second son, James, did not take up the sport of rodeo but that is just fine with Mom; he's busy driving machinery in the logging industry.

Joan believes the Creator does not send more hardships than a person can bear, but she has had more than her share of rough times. First there was the loss of her father and sister. Her husband, Bill, was killed in a logging accident in 1975. In June 1996, on Father's Day, son Wade died in a traffic accident, and within months, her mother, sister and nephew died from cancer.

Then she faced her own health issues and had to sell her cattle and most of her horses when she could no longer look after them. Worst of all, she could no longer ride. The animals and rodeo competition had been therapeutic for her, helping her over the dark times. "Horses were such a big part of my life. I cried when I saw the animals going," she says. "They keep you young at heart and provide therapy."

Then in August 2007, in the middle of her health problems, Joan's long-time home at Riske Creek burned to the ground and she lost everything in it, including Wade's pictures and trophies, her last tangible connection to him. As always, Joan met the troubles head on. She lived with brother Jack until she pulled herself together, then moved on, leaving Riske Creek and buying a place on the east side of the Fraser River. She has always loved to dance, and a few years ago she and friend Jean William saw competitive dancing at a powwow. Joan decided she would like to do that and she began competing at powwows.

Joan set 2012 as her year to retire, and in an unusual move, she gave the school district three years notice. Her reason? Her retirement was going to affect the budget she is responsible for, and she preferred to work it out over three school years than one.

Her plans for retirement include travel, enjoying her extended family, and dancing. Joan has received numerous honours, ranging from Williams Lake Citizen of the year to the BC Golden Jubilee award, and a BC rodeo lifetime achievement award. When she was notified in 1992 that she would receive the prestigious Order of BC, she was surprised to be told to wear a suit to the ceremony. She obliged, but the suit she wore was her buckskin outfit. Judge C.C. Barnett, one of her nominators for the OBC, noted Joan had "changed the stereotypical attitude that many white people held to aboriginals."

Joan says she's thankful for the people who have supported her through the trying times. "You realize who your true friends are."

Many of those true friends joined school district staff to honour her at her retirement party at Marie Sharpe elementary school on June 22, 2012.

4

MOTHERS AND DAUGHTERS

Vivien Cowan and Sonia Cornwall

The Grande Dames of Cariboo Art

*V*ivien Cowan and her daughter Sonia Cornwall were the grande dames of visual arts in the Cariboo. Had they been more interested in promoting themselves, or had they lived closer to a big city instead of the small town of Williams Lake, they might have been the grande dames of visual arts in all of Canada. They were also noteworthy members of the Cariboo ranching community.

Vivien Tully was born in St. Paul, Minnesota, in 1893 to Canadian parents. Her father was a banker. She was raised in Portland, Oregon, and Toronto before her family moved to Kamloops. There she met Irish adventurer and Boer War veteran Captain Charles Cowan. They were married in 1918 at the Douglas Lake Ranch.

Charles had guided British travellers through BC and later went into real estate. As an estate agent he managed a number of Cariboo ranches for absentee British gentry. He was a horse-and-buggy man, a dashing one to be sure, but he didn't drive motor vehicles. Vivien did, and after their marriage she chauffeured him around and about the countryside to oversee the ranch operations. She'd say, with a laugh, that she arrived in the Cariboo in a Cadillac. In 1920 the couple bought the historic Onward Ranch near 150 Mile House, just south of Williams Lake. In 1929 they added the neighbouring 150 Mile Ranch to their holdings.

The Onward was established during the Cariboo gold rush, and the huge ranch house, a mansion by Cariboo standards, was once a stopping house. It was rundown, but rather than replacing it, the Cowans spend five thousand dollars (a princely sum back then) on renovations, which included adding a sunroom and installing indoor plumbing. Water was stored in a big tank and the hired hands pumped water into it from the creek. There were four "lounges"—rooms that Vivien soon filled with antiques and artwork. The home became a treasury of books and paintings.

Vivien and Charles had two daughters, Sonia, born in 1919, and Drusilla, ten years later. The Cowans always had a live-in chef and housekeeper and they led a gracious and privileged lifestyle.

Many ranchers in the BC interior were British gentry, and they all knew the Cornwalls and often came to visit. The Onward was the scene of tennis games and outdoor teas in the summertime, and musical soirees all year round. Guests were treated to a traditional high tea at 4 p.m. Everyone dressed for the formal dinners, served at 7 p.m. The family spent the winter months in Victoria where they enjoyed city amenities and social life. Vivien took her linen, crystal and silverware with her for entertaining.

All was well until 1935 when Charles suffered a massive stroke. The family left the ranch in the capable hands of John Zirnhelt and moved to Victoria to be near medical care. When Charles died in 1939, Vivien returned to the Onward with the girls. Sonia, nineteen, was attending Strathcona Girl's School at the time. She had a promising career in fine arts ahead of her, but she came home to be a cowgirl. At the time, young ladies weren't encouraged to do ranch chores, as it was considered unseemly, but Sonia showed an interest in the outside work at an early age. She knew how to ride and rope, and she'd worked alongside the men driving the tractor, putting up hay, building fences, rounding up cattle, and doing whatever was required. When she came home after her father died, the Onward crew accepted her help and treated her as an equal.

Vivien had a good grip on ranch management but the dirty thirties had been hard on ranchers and Charles' illness had been costly. There wasn't much cash around, but the ranch had a huge garden, and the family was self-sufficient when it came to food. They even grew wheat, which was milled at Soda Creek. In the winter, Sonia trapped furs to sell for cigarette money. Vivien found the money to send Dru to boarding school in Naramata and later to Strathcona.

Vivien had always been interested in painting but she had no training. In 1943, when finances were healthier, she remedied that and went to the Banff School of Fine Arts. One of her instructors there was A.Y. Jackson, the legendary Canadian artist and member of the famed Group of Seven. Jackson was intrigued by Vivien's descriptions of a working ranch in the Cariboo, and when she invited him to visit the Onward, he was quick to accept. He returned many times to paint and to explore the countryside. In 1945, when Vivien founded the Cariboo Art Society, based at the Onward, Jackson agreed to be honourary life president. The society is still going strong. It is believed to be one of the oldest, if not the oldest, continuing art society in BC.

Vivien's interest in the arts, combined with her hospitality, led to the Onward Ranch becoming the centre for an artists' residency program. Visiting artists spent a few days or a few weeks at the ranch, where along with painting they took part in a number of activities including print-making, weaving, pottery and sculpture. Like Jackson, they enjoyed exploring the countryside and meeting and mingling with cowboys, members of the arts society and residents of the neighbouring

When Vivien Cowan was widowed with two young daughters, she opted to run the ranch rather than sell it. She was an efficient businesswoman, but left the ranching part of the operation to foreman John Zirnhelt and daughter Sonia.

Sugar Cane First Nations community. Locals had the opportunity to meet many prominent artists, including Zelko Kujundzic, founder of the Kootenay School of the Arts, Lilias Torrance Newton, Joseph Plaskett, Takao Tanabe, Molly Bobak, Herbert Siebner and Jack Hardman.

When Sonia was a child, Vivien turned the attic into a studio and gave her an easel and paints to keep her busy when the weather kept her indoors. Sonia was always part of the Onward arts community, and she too became a friend of A.Y. Jackson. She painted when she could but ranch duties really didn't leave much time for it. In 1946 Vivien sent both daughters off to the Provincial Institute of Technology in Calgary to study art. They were supposed to be there for a year, but they didn't like the city life nor the restrictions of the institute's programs. They lasted three months and came home.

The next year, Sonia married Hugh Cornwall

Vivien studied with A.Y. Jackson at the Banff School of Fine Arts in 1943.

and the couple took over management of the 150 Mile Ranch. Hugh, who had served in the RAF during the war, was the grandson of Clement Cornwall, a prominent pioneer rancher in the Ashcroft area. After the war Hugh played a major role in marketing for the Cariboo Cattlemen. He was fieldman with the BC Livestock Co-op when he and Sonia wed. They managed the 150 Mile operation until it was sold in 1950, then managed the Onward until 1965 when it was sold to the Roman Catholic Oblate Brothers who operated nearby St. Joseph's Mission. The Cornwalls moved to Jones Lake where they established their own ranch on pastures and hay meadows that were part of the original Onward holdings.

Vivien enjoyed travelling, and she and Dru spent time in Africa and then went to England, where Dru was formally presented to King George VI. When she left Onward, Vivien moved to a home beside Williams Lake where she continued to paint and study. She attended many workshops and institutes,

Sonia was not only an artist of some renown, she was a "working" rancher, taking an active part in ranch chores, handling cattle as well as working with ranch-related organizations. Part of ranching was feeding everybody who happened to come by, and Sonia excelled at that too.

including the San Miguel Institute in Mexico, and for a number of years she went to the Nelson School of Fine Arts.

Vivien died in 1990 at the age of ninety-seven. Her paintings live on.

Along with a reputation for being fiercely independent, Cariboo ranchers were known for their hospitality. Like her mother, Sonia could have written the book on the subject. She extended a warm and gracious welcome to everyone who appeared on her doorstep, providing nourishment for both soul and body with good conversation, good company and good food. She could cope with any number of unexpected guests arriving at mealtime without batting an eye. She always had something baked fresh out of the oven.

Branding was a special event at Jones Lake. All and sundry were invited to participate in both the branding and Sonia's meals. Another social tradition was the annual duck hunt. In September, on the first day of hunting, Hugh's cronies gathered in the morning for the shoot. At noon the hunters would retire to the ranch house where Sonia would have lunch, often freshly baked corn bread and baked beans, along with some liquid refreshment. On Boxing Day, the Cornwalls held an open house.

Both Hugh and Sonia were deeply involved with both local and provincial cattlemen's associations. Sonia clerked for auctioneers and brand inspectors at cattle sales. At one bull sale in Kamloops, when the committee organizing the after-sale event realized they had no decorations, Sonia commandeered some sheets of plywood and painted appropriate background scenery on them. The panels are currently on display at the Museum of the Cariboo Chilcotin, which is also home to a number of her paintings.

The Onward Ranch and the ranch house date back to Cariboo gold rush days. The stately home was the scene of much social activity during the years the Cowans were in residence.

Sonia Cowan Cornwall painted what she knew best, Cariboo people and the countryside. She recorded the ranching history through her paintings.

For years Sonia simply didn't have time to paint, but when daughters Mabel and Mary started school, she picked up the brushes again. Although getting off to a relatively late start, she became one of BC's outstanding artists.

Sonia lived at 150 Mile House for most of her life, and she painted the world she loved and lived in. Holiday trips to Fiji and Mexico resulted in some brilliant canvases, and she is best known for her paintings of working cowboys, ranchers and her beloved Cariboo landscape. She had no formal training, and while she was influenced by the French Impressionists and the Group of Seven (thanks to her friendship with A.Y. Jackson) she had her own distinctive impressionist style. She often painted to the music of the Beatles.

Sonia was a charter member of Cariboo Arts Society, and served a number of years as chair. In 1981 she co-founded the Station House Gallery, which in later years hosted a number of her shows. Her work was known all over Canada. She had one-woman shows in Vancouver, Victoria and Kamloops. Her paintings always sold well, but she painted mostly for her own enjoyment.

The Cornwalls had a deep interest in the history of their families and the BC cattle industry. Their collection of books, archives and artifacts was so large it was housed in a special building on the ranch. Sonia not only let interested visitors browse in this family museum, she fed them while they were at it. When Hugh died in 2001, Sonia remained at Jones Lake.

The Cornwalls left big footprints. Their contributions to the ranching and arts communities, and to the Cariboo at large, earned them a place in the Cowboy Hall of Fame. Sonia accepted the induction in 2005. She died the next year, shortly after returning from a trip to Mexico. At her memorial service, many of her paintings were on display along with her well-worn saddle, chaps and riding boots. The Cariboo art community honoured her by instituting a scholarship to the Island Mountain School of Arts.

Cathy, Robin and Crystal Verhaeghe

Education Is the Key

When Cathy Baptiste (Verhaeghe) was fourteen, she went to a private Christian school in Palmer, Alaska. It was not only a grand adventure for a country girl, it changed the direction of her life. The school gave her structure, discipline, respect and a goal.

Cathy spent her early years at Mountain House, a small homestead on the south side of Chilko River in the Chilcotin country. The place belonged to her grandfather, Eagle Lake Henry, a well-known and respected rancher, guide and trapper who had given up his First Nations status for what was then called "white rights." He and his wife, Ellietta, adopted Cathy's mother, Donna. Donna had a traditional upbringing, but unfortunately she didn't pass her knowledge on to the children. Cathy's dad, Gabriel Baptiste, was a member of the Alexandria Band. He'd gone to St. Joseph's Mission where he was a hockey and boxing star. He too was enfranchised, so Donna lost her status when they married.

Photo above: L-R Robin, Cathy and Crystal.

Cathy is the fifth-oldest of the thirteen Baptiste children. There were ten girls and three boys. She remembers the Henry ranch as a wonderful place for youngsters, and Eagle Lake himself was a strong influence in their lives. They had horses to ride and the lake to play in. The family camped in the summer in the hayfields, and spent the winters in the small cabin on the homestead. Gabriel bought the children skates so they could share his passion for hockey and in the winter members of the small community gathered to play the game in a cleared rink on a lake. In the spring everyone in the valley took part in gymkhanas.

"We wandered all over the place," Cathy remembers. "We played in the lake although none of us could swim, and no one seemed to worry about bears getting us."

When the oldest children were school age, the Baptistes rented a house for them about one and a half kilometres from the Tatla Lake School. Lorene, thirteen, the oldest daughter, looked after them. She cooked and did everything and went to school too. Cathy remembers having hassles at school from the "white kids" but one teacher, the late Louise Satre, didn't put up with any nonsense from anyone.

All was well until November1964, when Gabriel died in a car accident. Donna was pregnant, and she had a hard time coping without him. In the fall of 1965 she moved to Williams Lake with the children and began drinking. Cathy says their rented house became the biggest party home in Williams Lake.

In the spring of 1966, Cathy, twelve, and her sister Ida, thirteen, cornered their mother and said they wanted to go home to their cabin in Tatlayoko. Donna agreed, saying if they packed everything, she'd take them home. She did, but much to their surprise she dropped them off at the cabin and left them with the six younger children and the baby to look after. She also left her stick-shift pickup truck.

"For childcare, Ida would go to school for two days a week and I would go three days," Cathy explains. "Eventually Ida dropped out."

Cathy says she doesn't know the details, but Donna had made arrangements with the proprietor of the Tatla Lake general store to provide food for the children and said she would settle the bill. "Once a week we put a food order in at the post office, and in the middle of the week our food would come. The post office was about five miles up the valley so I learned how to drive Mom's truck to pick up the groceries."

This arrangement was especially hard on the younger children. That winter the baby became ill. Cathy and a neighbour went to the Bracewell Ranch for help, and Gerry Bracewell told them a family was going to Williams Lake that night. She also invited them all to her house for Christmas dinner. Cathy went to Williams Lake with the baby and stayed with relatives while she was in hospital, but because she was underage, she wasn't allowed to take the baby home. The little one went into foster care until she was two and a half.

In 1968, Donna moved to Puntzi Mountain with the younger children. The Arctic Missions had a Christian outreach program for Native Indians in Canada, and a couple of families came to Puntzi, where Cathy met them. "They asked if I wanted to go to school in Alaska, and I did, so my mother gave permission for me to go. I was only gone for the one year."

She travelled by plane from Seattle to Anchorage, quite an experience for a fourteen-year-old country girl. "We learned to get up early, go to school and wash our clothes. We all had chores. Mine was scrubbing the bathroom and showers in the girl's dormitory. I had never been to a dentist before and all of my teeth were fixed in Anchorage. Social studies was a challenge, learning fifty-one states instead of ten provinces, but I'm still in awe when I hear the 'Star-Spangled Banner.'"

The experience effected her deeply. She decided she was never going to live in a home where alcohol ruled, and she realized that to make that happen, she had to further her education.

When Cathy and Ida were ready for high school, Donna got them a ride to town on a logging truck but then they were on their own. They managed to get themselves enrolled at Williams Lake Junior Secondary and into the dormitory. They had no way to get home for holidays but Grandma and Grandpa Baptiste lived at Castle Rock so they went there. Cathy's heritage is Carrier, Chilcotin and Shuswap. "Most of the First Nations students thought we were Shuswap, and for a time I didn't know where I belonged."

Eagle Lake Henry had always been an example for Cathy. She was in Grade 9 when he was brought to the hospital in Williams Lake. When she visited him, he asked her in English if she spoke her language. "I hung my head and said no," Cathy says. A few days later he died.

Cathy spent a year in Prince George, then came back to graduate from Columneetza. In 1973 she went to Cariboo College in Kamloops where she took her first year in arts, then came back to Williams Lake to work for Silvacan. There she met Herve Verhaeghe, who worked as a Cat operator for his Uncle Gabe Pinette, who owned Silvacan. They married in 1974. Herve was from Ste. Rose du Lac, Manitoba. He came from a good home and a strong Catholic upbringing. He was no stranger to work, and as a child he'd helped with the farming chores. In 1977 he started his own business in general construction. He's built a number of homes, some from his own blueprints.

Cathy and Herve have two daughters, Robin and Crystal. Cathy stayed home with them until the economy took a dip in 1980. There wasn't much construction work, so she went back to work, first for the Alexis Creek Band at Redstone, then with the Canoe Creek Band. She put in long days driving back and forth to both places. Crystal went to Redstone with her and went to kindergarten there. It was the only time she felt "different." Her red hair did make her feel like the odd person out.

Herve always shared the job of parenting, and he looked after Robin when Cathy and Crystal were going to Redstone. He is bilingual; his elementary school was taught in French, high school in English. He often sang "Alouette" to the girls in French. He is a kind man, but he was strict with the girls. They say it's a different story with the grandchildren.

Cathy felt her office skills were limited, so she took office upgrading at evening courses before she went to work for the Cariboo Tribal Council (CTC) in 1980. At the time, all fifteen First Nations Bands in the Cariboo Chilcotin belonged to the CTC. Now there are three separate groups. Cathy, Robin and Crystal are members of the Alexandria (Esdilagh) Band.

Cathy and Herve expected the girls to do well and they did. Both went to Chilcotin Road Elementary, Anne Stevenson Junior Secondary, and they graduated from Columneetza. It didn't occur to either of them that they wouldn't go to university. Robin says her choice of a career in medicine was triggered by a visit to Dr. Dennis Sokol's office in Williams Lake. She was impressed and made up her mind to be a doctor. It is probably coincidental that she chose to specialize in obstetrics, but her grandmother Donna was a midwife. Robin took her bachelor of science degree with a major in biology at the University of Victoria in 1997 and graduated from the University of British Columbia Medical School in 2001. She was the fifth BC First Nation graduate from UBC's medical school.

Robin met Robert Johnson at a conference for aboriginal medical students in Winnipeg when she was a first-year medical student. Robert, who was raised on the Millbrook Mi'kmag First Nation in Nova Scotia, was in his fourth-year medicine at Dalhousie University in Halifax. They were married in 2000 at the 108 Mile, and they went back to Nova Scotia where Robin began her five-year post-graduate studies at Dalhousie.

On a visit to Williams Lake in 2005, Robin and Robert did some "holiday" work at Cariboo Memorial Hospital (CMH). Robert was used to working in emergency rooms in large hospitals and he liked the slower pace at CMH. He wanted to stay. Robin was all for coming home, so he stayed at CMH, keeping three-year-old son, Reese, with him while she returned to Dalhousie. When her studies were completed there was an opening for a gynecologist/obstetrician at CMH, so the Johnsons were in Williams Lake to stay.

Since then Robert has served as chief of staff and he took a year off in 2010/11 to train as an anesthesiologist. Since coming to Williams Lake, the Johnson family has grown with another son, Kyle, and daughter, Kelsey. With a demanding job, Robin is always on call, and with three young children, she doesn't have much time for community activities.

After Columneetza, Crystal went to Mount Royal College in Calgary, graduating from the Small Business and Entrepreneurship Degree Program in 2000. She moved to Vancouver to take New Media CD Rom and Web Development at BCIT. In 2002 she opened her own company, Emoda Design, in Williams Lake. When she decided to continue her education, she went to UNBC, graduating in 2006 with an Executive MBA. She went to work for the Tsilhqot'in National Government (TNG) as the economic development officer, and in 2009 she became the TNG's executive director. Crystal loves her job, as she says she's doing work she believes in: "The TNG isn't a corporation, we're a government for the people."

She taught management and computer courses for the Weekend University at Thompson Rivers University (TRU) in Williams Lake, and she continues to do website development. In her spare time she is a mountain biker, and that's how she met Tony Emard, who was working at Red Shreds. They were married in September 2011 at Patricia Lake, Alberta. Herve built them a house, not far from the Verhaeghe home, and Tony is currently working for Herve as a carpenter's apprentice.

Crystal is an excellent cook. She reads cookbooks and is always trying new things. During harvest time, she and Cathy can fruit and vegetables.

Cathy got her university degree the hard way. She says the opportunity of a lifetime came in 1997 with the opening of the Cariboo Chilcotin Weekend University. While working full-time, she took courses every second Friday and Saturday for seven years, and spent July on campus at TRU or UNBC. She says one of her toughest professors was daughter Crystal.

The weekend university, which closed in 2011, was founded by Sister Mary Alice Danaher and Bruce Mack. Cathy and Don Dixon from Canim Lake were the first graduates in 2004. In October 2010, Cathy received her Accounting Technician Diploma from TRU in Kamloops.

Cathy and Herve enjoy the outdoors, camping and hunting. They like to travel and, of course, they enjoy their family. "We've had a few dark patches in our lives that built our characters and the will to survive," Cathy says. "Could we live in a cabin with no running water and an outhouse today? Sure."

Donna eventually did stop drinking, much to the joy of her children. "We had several good years with her until she passed away in 2000." Cathy says, "I believe there was no support system for her to deal with grief and being a single mom," Cathy says. "Two of my older sisters worked for BC Tel for thirty-five years until they retired, Ida worked for the provincial government for thirty-five years, and our baby sister is alive and well and cooking for a restaurant in Whitehorse."

As for Cathy, Robin and Crystal, it would be hard to find better role models for First Nations' women on the Cariboo Chilcotin no matter what their age.

Phyllis and Ivy Chelsea

The Fight for Sobriety

The story has been often told of the small girl who was the catalyst for setting an entire village on the path to sobriety. This is how it happened.

On a July weekend in 1972, Phyllis Chelsea left her three children, Ivy, Dean and Robert, with her mother, Lily Squinahan, who lived on the Alkali Lake Indian Reserve. The children often stayed with their grandmother while Phyllis and her husband, Andy, went on weekend binges. This time, when Phyllis, hungover and feeling ill, dragged herself to fetch the children, Ivy wouldn't go with her.

"I'm not going home, you guys drink too much," she told her mother. Phyllis was so shocked she never did have another drink. Andy went on the wagon a few days later.

At the time of Ivy's rebellion, the village of Alkali Lake (Esket), fifty kilometres south of Williams Lake, was home to some four hundred people belonging to the Shuswap (Secwepemc) nation. Locals called it Alcohol Lake, with good reason. Most of the adult residents were drunks. It was a sad place. Phyllis describes it as a hellhole. Houses, built by the Department of Indian Affairs and tacky at the best of times, were falling apart. Children were hungry, neglected and often abused. There were all kinds of crimes, all alcohol-related. Almost all the families were on social assistance.

When people are dependent on alcohol, they don't care about much of anything except where the next drink is coming from, but Phyllis and Andy decided if they could beat the booze, others could too. They set about making that happen.

Phyllis is physically small. She has an infectious laugh, a broad sense of humour, and more than her share of energy and courage, and that saw her through some tough times. She grew up on one of the reserve meadows, away from the village, where her parents raised horses and cattle. They only went to Esket for church or other celebrations. She went to St. Joseph's Mission until she was six-teen, and she does not have good memories of that. Her dad, Pierro Squinahan, was a well-known horseman and a champion Mountain Race winner at the Williams Lake Stampedes. Phyllis was the Indian Stampede Queen in 1963.

When Phyllis and Andy Chelsea overcame their addiction to alcohol, they figured others could do it too, and they spent the next twenty years working to improve both the social and economic situations at the Esket community.

She and Andy were married in 1964. Andy grew up at Gang Ranch, and he too attended St. Joseph's, but he ran away. When they stopped drinking, he was work-ing at a sawmill at Springhouse. He had a reputation as a hard worker, but like most of their generation, he and Phyllis started hitting the bottle as teenagers. "Everyone did," Phyllis says.

Once they decided to bring sobriety to the community, there was no turning back. Their goal was to have a village where everyone was sober and gainfully em-ployed. They were convinced the dependency on welfare money was one cause of the drinking problems.

Andy ran for, and was elected chief of the band council, and he used the power of that position to bring about reform. One of his first moves was to appoint Phyllis as the band's social worker.

For the first few years they were the only ones sober. Then Mable Johnson (Paul) joined them and later Laura Harry. Encouraging them along the way was Alan Haig-Brown, a local teacher, and later Indian education coordinator for School District #27. It was not smooth going. They were met with resistance, resentment, hostility and even threats.

Andy is a big man, and fearless. Phyllis wasn't always fearless, but she did what she had to do. While Andy focused on economic development, Phyllis took on

Ivy Chelsea is the mother of five and grand-mother of four. When she isn't teaching she's travelling with Letwilc, a four-day program focusing on healing and building self-esteem. Along with all that she is working on her master's degree from the University of Northern BC.

the social problems. Her job as social worker got off to a rocky start when the Department of Indian Affairs questioned her qualifications for the post. Once that was settled, she set to work. Over the next seventeen years she was the moving force behind many changes.

One of the first changes the Chelseas made was giving out food vouchers instead of welfare cheques so the money didn't go to buying booze. When the nearest store wouldn't take the vouchers, Phyllis and Evelyn Ignatius opened a store on the reserve, called P&E Store. Under Phyllis' guidance, the band established a nursery school and a homemaker's club. A number of children had no parents, so she started a group home. Along with everything else, she acted as a liaison between the different agencies and the reserve. "I wrote endless reports," she recalls.

The band convinced DIA to hand over the administration of the social agencies so they could be staffed with band members. The latter, being in touch with local traditions, provided better service.

The well-being of the children was a major concern. Gaining sobriety meant involving the whole family, but it was several years before a significant number of parents were sober. Phyllis found room in her home and heart to take in dozens of abused and neglected youngsters. All this was in addition to her own family, which was joined by two more sons, Kevin and Snewt.

Education was another worry. Esketemc children weren't doing well in public schools. Looking for an answer, Phyllis ran for and was elected to the Cariboo Chilcotin School Board. She was the district's first First Nations trustee, and she met with some discrimination. The first time she went to Vancouver to represent the board at a meeting, the hotel clerk wouldn't believe she was a trustee and didn't want to honour her room reservation.

She was instrumental in having the school district form an Indian Education Committee and hire a coordinator and this has grown into a full-fledged district department. In the end, though, she found the best solution to the education issue was for the band to have its own school. The band was given control of the federal education funding and established Sxoxomic Elementary School (now K to 10) at

Ivy, her youngest daughter, Carmen, and Phyllis enjoy a campfire in the backyard of the Chelsea home at Alkali Lake.

Esket in 1975. The first principal, John Rathjen, was exactly the right person for the job. He was loved and respected by all, especially the students, and he got the school off to a good start, but then tragedy hit. John lost his life during a Halloween gathering at the lake. Martin Reidemann, the owner of the Alkali Lake Ranch, was in a boat on the lake setting off fireworks to entertain the children when a gust of wind toppled the boat. John swam out to rescue him but both men perished in the cold water.

The Chelseas knew first-hand that the residential school experiences were a root cause of alcoholism. Secwepemc family values, language, spiritual and cultural traditions along with pride in their heritage had been lost to an entire generation. A key to recovery was the revival of these traditions. Phyllis saw that the Shuswap language was taught not only at Sxoxomic but also in the area's public schools, and it became recognized for credit at UBC. Sweat lodges were revived along with Secwepemc songs, drumming, arts and crafts and knowledge of plants and medicines.

Nothing happened overnight. People became sober almost one by one until 1978. As more band members came home from rehabilitation centres to remodelled houses, happy children and jobs, they started a chain reaction and many others decided to go to treatment too. It became socially unacceptable to be a boozer.

Thanks to the economic development plan, there was a variety of available jobs, including logging, construction, ranching and gardening, and there was a safety net of support to help people stay sober. By 1979 the Esket population was about 98 percent dry. It was a remarkable turnaround.

Phyllis took on other challenges. Over the years she was a homeschool coordinator, a court worker, a language teacher (she co-authored two books on learning Shuswap), and above all she was an example. She really enjoyed court work and would have liked to go into law but that wasn't in the works.

Esket was well on the path to sobriety when the Chelseas suffered a personal loss. Their son Dean lost a battle with diabetes and died in 1981. His death triggered an interest in spirituality among the younger people. "That's where we had support," Phyllis says. "So many of the elders were burned out."

Word of the Alkali achievements caught the attention of groups like the Four World International Institute. In 1985 a film, *The Honour of All: The Story of Alkali Lake,* told how it all came about. As a result of the film, Phyllis and Andy began conducting workshops and training sessions in other communities. Their work was and still is recognized in Canada, the United States and Australia.

Along the way, Phyllis took numerous university courses and served on many boards and agencies. She also received several prestigious awards including two of BC's top honours. In May 1989, she received an honourary Doctor of Laws from UBC for her "gentle courage and dedication in the pursuit of a better life for herself, her family and her community. Through her stubborn refusal to accept institutional assistance, she fostered among her people long dormant feelings of pride and self-reliance."

In June 1990, she received the Order of BC. The citation noted her courage to stay sober when all around her were not. It said "as a community leader, mother, grandmother, and now a great-grandmother, Phyllis has given inspiration, hope and support to all who have known her."

Phyllis is now retired, kind of. She and Andy live on small acreage several kilometres from the Esket village. Phyllis suffers from osteoporosis but that doesn't stop her from teaching Secwepemc language and culture at local schools when required, nor from becoming involved in political controversies, such as the Indian Residential School claims. She, Andy and Ivy still travel to provide training and workshops, and Phyllis continually gets phone calls and emails from recovering alcoholics looking for support.

And what about Ivy, who started it all?

Ivy is the single mother of five grown children and grandmother of four. She is a teacher, a facilitator and a trainer. She went through a rough patch as a teenager; she was pregnant at sixteen, and fell off the wagon shortly after her daughter was born. She did all the things she'd objected to her parents doing, and ended up in hospital. With her mother's help she got back on track, but then had a difficult marriage. She picked up the pieces, went back to school, and received her bachelor of arts from the University of Northern BC with a major in First Nations studies. She is currently teaching for the Prince George School District while working on her master's degree.

She's travelled all over North America with her mother, and sometimes her dad, with Letwilc (translation: from the heart) a four-day program modelled on New Directions. It focuses on healing and building self-esteem. In July 2010, the trio were honoured by the San Carlos Apache Tribe in Arizona. Ivy believes strong communities are made up of strong individuals, and Letwilc teaches people to be strong.

Recalling her childhood days at Esket, Ivy says she and her brothers were never physically abused, but many of their schoolmates were. She says what made a big difference for the young people was the establishment of Sxoxomic and the influence of John Rathjen.

Esket is not entirely alcohol-free today. One generation beat the habit (and is still sober) but some of the current generation are wrestling with addictions. However, Esket is a very different place now than it was in the 1970s. It is a happy place where people are proud of themselves and their accomplishments.

Page 166: L-R Phyllis and Ivy Chelsea. Photo of Ivy taken by Remington John Photography.

Nancy and Shirley-Pat Gale

The Apple Falls Close to the Tree

ancy Gale and her daughter, Shirley-Pat Gale, are relative newcomers to the Cariboo Chilcotin. Nancy, who is best known for her work with the Child Development Centre and her commitment to the community, arrived in Williams Lake in 1995 to work for the Business Development Bank. Shirley-Pat is also making her mark in the community. She came to Williams Lake in 2005 to stay with her family while she completed her master's thesis. She became involved in some of her mother's projects, found work she enjoys, a man she loves, and is making Williams Lake her home. Like Nancy, she is an active volunteer and believes in "getting things done."

Nancy was a single mom living in Thunder Bay, Ontario, when she met Gary Gale. He was a single dad and his son, Brian, and Shirley-Pat attended the same daycare centre. The centre manager got them together and they became friends. When Brian's son later went to Newfoundland and couldn't take his dog, Nancy ended up with it, and says she got the dog first, Gary and Brian later. Both children approved, and Nancy and Gary were married in 1983.

They later moved to Marathon, Ontario, where Shirley-Pat took up figure skating. She had a skating partner in Enderby, BC, and a visit to that community resulted in the Gales moving to the Okanagan town. Shirley-Pat attended high school there, and Nancy worked for the Haney Heritage House in Salmon Arm where she did the marketing and put on events.

A figure skater's life isn't easy, and neither is that of the figure skater's mother. Nancy and Shirley-Pat were up at 4 a.m. so they could get to the arena in Vernon for lessons. Shirley-Pat was intent on being a competitive figure skater, and when she graduated from high school, Nancy gave her one year to focus on skating, and then it was back to school "no matter what." Shirley-Pat went to Montreal and began training.

As a youngster, Nancy Gale was a dancer.

With Shirley-Pat gone, Nancy was ready for a move. The Business Development Bank (BDB) was advertising positions in Peace River, Cranbrook and Williams Lake. Nancy applied, and was offered the Williams Lake position.

"When I arrived and saw cowboy hats and lassos on the street signs I did wonder what I was getting into," she says. She brought a wealth of experience to the job, as she had an impressive background as a business consultant and municipal employee in Ontario.

The job with the BDB introduced her to the movers and shakers in Williams Lake, but it wasn't what she'd expected. In 1996 she went to the newly established Community Skills Centre as Manager/ Education Coordinator. The centre, one of twenty established in 1995, was to partner with businesses, colleges, schools and non-profit organizations to provide easily accessible upgrading and skills training for adults. Nancy says it was an excellent concept but the provincial funding lasted only five years. For a variety of reasons, the Williams Lake centre was one of the sixteen that didn't survive. In 2000, Nancy accepted a position with the Cariboo Chilcotin Child Development (CDC) and became executive director.

In the meantime, Shirley-Pat had given up on figure skating. "I had a good shot at winning," she says, "but one morning I woke up and wondered what I was doing. I had no life outside the arena. Of thirty skating students, only two of us had a high school diploma."

So, before the championships, she hung up her skates, and enrolled at Concordia University where she took a double major: history, and classical languages and literature.

Shirley-Pat took dancing lessons along with figure skating.

If Nancy had believed Shirley-Pat's Grade 3 teacher, her daughter would never have been eligible for university. The teacher said Shirley-Pat was dyslexic, stupid, and would never get anywhere academically. Nancy accepted dyslexic, but not the rest of it, and she was right. Shirley-Pat didn't accept her dyslexia as an excuse either, but she says she wouldn't have made it without an advocate—her mom. "It's amazing what having confidence can do for you," she says.

Not surprisingly, both mother and daughter have a huge interest in making sure everyone has a chance to an education regardless of labels. After graduating from Concordia in 2000, Shirley-Pat "ran away" and travelled in Asia, teaching English as a second language.

Back in Williams Lake, Nancy took the positive aspects of the skills centre with her as a template for reorganizing the CDC. Under her direction values were refocused on family-directed care and community relationships. She developed a service delivery system that begins and ends with the parents' goals for their children and their families. Client information management systems were redesigned so managers build and maintain relationships with families, staff and community partners. "The secret of our success is teamwork," Nancy says.

Under her direction, the CDC's income grew from $0.9 million to over $2 million and the centre delivers a wide range of services including speech and language therapy, intensive support and supervision (youth justice), pre-natal, child and youth mental health services, FASD (fetal alcohol) Key Worker and Family Support services and Youth Forensics.

Nancy's belief in taking down walls led to the CDC becoming a founding member agency of the Central Interior Community Services Co-operative. The Co-op houses a number of community social services agencies which share resources in a new building in the downtown area. The original CDC building has been renovated and with the support of community donors, corporate sponsors and foundations, $116,000 was raised to rehabilitate the playground area to improve accessibility.

Nancy had a BA Honours in Sociology (1975) from Carlton University, along with many other qualifications, but in the late 1990s she decided to get her master's degree. She received a Master of Continuing Education, specializing in Workplace Learning, from the University of Calgary in 2004.

Her work with the CDC covers a wide range of activities locally and provincially, and her community work includes, but is not limited to, involvement with Williams Lake's Business Improvement Association and the Daybreak Rotary Club of Williams Lake. She is past president of the club, and one of her activities has been as parade organizer and marshal for the Williams Lake Stampede parade. Organizing this event is a major task.

Shirley-Pat returned to BC after nine years away and enrolled at the University of Victoria for a master of Education in Leadership Studies. Her thesis focused on whistle-blowing. She'd had personal experience in this area, starting in Grade 12 when she blew the whistle on her high school principal and counsellor for unfairness in a school election. In Japan she took on a teacher who hit a student. She believes the right to blow the whistle on wrongdoings is an important one in the pursuit of doing real good.

When she came to Williams Lake, Nancy got her involved in this and that. One "this" was compiling the research Nancy had done on social services for the Cariboo Chilcotin Beetle Action Coalition. One of the "thats" was getting involved in the Daybreak Rotary Club of Williams Lake. Along the way Shirley-Pat met Bruce Mack, who got her interested in literacy in Williams Lake. She became program coordinator for Partners in Assisted Learning (PAL) from 2007 to 2011. Her resume is impressive and includes consulting and proposal writing and she was also a sessional instructor for both UNBC and TRU. And she met the man in her life, Dwayne Chamberlain. The two have a house, a dog and wedding plans.

Nancy has received numerous awards in recognition of her work on the job and in the community. They include the 2005 Community Booster Award from the Williams Lake and District Chamber of Commerce, the 2007 BC Psychologically Healthy Workplace Award for small not-for-profit organizations and Rotary International's Paul Harris Fellow Award from the Daybreak Rotary Club of Williams Lake in 2007.

Nancy served as both secretary and president of the Daybreak Rotary. Shirley-Pat was elected to position of president of the group in 2010 and is currently serving for 2011–2012. In her early thirties, she is the youngest member and youngest local president. She believes it is important to use the strength of organizations to help communities. She is the ambassador for the Government House and Rotary International Joint Literacy Project, a project that establishes literacy opportunities (i.e. libraries) in remote communities. Shirley-Pat realized this project could be done "in our own backyards." Her work with PAL included working with First Nations, and she put the two together to establish a library at Tl'esqox (Toosey) in June 2011. She says it has been an honour and a joy working with Lieutenant-Governor Stephen Point. As for Toosey, the band council adopted her—one of her greatest honours.

In March 2012, Lieutenant-Governor Steven Point recommended her, and Shirley-Pat was chosen as one of the BC residents to be honoured with the Queen Elizabeth II Diamond Jubilee medal for her outstanding work in promoting literacy.

Along with working for the same goals, the mother/daughter team share an interest in travelling and learning, and they often travel together. They have visited Greece, Italy, the British Isles, France, Holland, Spain and Cuba. In 2010 they went to Oxford together and took a course on music, language and the brain. The two look forward to future adventures.

Adaline and Cathie Hamm

Pharmacy Isn't Just About Medicine—It's About People

For Adaline Hamm, being a pharmacist was doing what she loved, and loving what she did. Daughter Cathie feels the same way. Addie, as Adaline is affectionately known, was a pharmacist in Williams Lake for over forty-five years, thirty years as partner in Kornak and Hamm's Pharmacy, the business she started in 1981. She is known for going that extra mile with customers, and taking time to deal with each one personally. Daughter Cathie, who is now the company's president and pharmacy manager, has followed in her mom's footsteps.

Adaline came to Williams Lake in 1962 when her husband, Martin, accepted a job as supervisor of elementary instruction with School District #27. The couple and their three sons were living in Chilliwack, where Martin was teaching and Addie was working part-time as a pharmacist, when the job offer came. Martin wasn't particularly excited about the move but Addie was all in favour. "I was tired of the city," she says. "And I was tired of the rain and constantly having to change the boys into dry clothes."

Addie was born and spent her early years on Vancouver Island. Her family moved to New Westminster in the 1930s when her father took a job with the penitentiary there. She wanted to be a nurse but, having had tuberculosis when she was a teenager, she couldn't risk further exposure in direct patient care, so she went into pharmacy instead. She apprenticed at St. Paul's Hospital in Vancouver, then attended the University of British Columbia for the three-year program. It was mostly a man's field at the time; she was one of only eight women in a class of fifty. After graduation she wanted to leave the Greater Vancouver area, so she took a job at Lock's Pharmacy in Chilliwack. It was a good choice.

Martin was teaching in Chilliwack, and they met at a bowling alley. They married in 1954. Addie worked full-time until Ernie was born in 1955, and later she was often called in for part-time work. She says when she was pregnant she wore a big white smock so no one would notice. Rob was born in 1957 and Brian in 1959.

Addie hadn't planned on working in Williams Lake but pharmacists were in short supply, and Cariboo Memorial Hospital was in dire straits. The hospital board pleaded with her, and she agreed to work part-time providing she could work around spending time with the boys.

"They told me I could come in the middle of the night if I wanted to," she says. She took the job and set up the pharmacy's formulary and clinical services. She later set up the 100 Mile House Hospital's pharmacy as well.

Cathie was born in 1965, and Addie had to work around having a young child, sometimes taking the baby to work. With the encouragement of the hospital administrator, she had taken some courses, and she was enjoying the work, when in

After some years working for other people, pharmacist Adaline Hamm wanted to start her own pharmacy. Colleague Harry Kornak had the same idea so in May 1981, they opened Kornak and Hamm Pharmacists Ltd. The business, located at 366 Yorston Street. in downtown Williams Lake, is still going strong.

the late 1960s, the hospital board and some of the doctors had a disagreement. This resulted in major turmoil, and the administrator was dismissed. The new administrator wanted a full-time pharmacist and advertised for one without telling Addie. When she learned of this, she threw in her keys and went home. Board members talked her into returning, so she stayed until they found a full-time person, then left for good.

She wasn't unemployed for long. She worked for Cunningham Drugs, then the Spencer-Dickie drugstore. She enjoyed being in retail pharmacy again, with direct patient contact, but she was frustrated by the pressures of working for others and not being able to practise her ideals. She was on the Council of the College of Pharmacists at the time, and council members encouraged her to start her own store. When she saw a building going up at 366 Yorston Street, across the street from the Yorston Medical building, she saw it was the ideal location for a new pharmacy.

Harry Kornak, a fellow employee, agreed to be a partner in a new business. Addie was all set to go when she ran into a snag. No bank would lend her money. They said she had no collateral and they considered a woman to be a poor risk. She finally borrowed money from a relative, and the success of the business proved the naysayers wrong. Business was slow at first, but Addie was encouraged by long-time doctor and friend Hugh Atwood, who said she'd do well with people who knew her. That's what happened. By the second year the business was thriving. When the business celebrated its thirtieth birthday in 2011, many who came to the party were original customers. "We've always had a great clientele," Addie says.

It wasn't always easy. There were worries when Overwaitea opened a pharmacy in 1986, but within a few months their business was as strong as before and still growing. At the same time, Shoppers Drug Mart closed its Boitanio Mall store and bought out Spencer-Dickie downtown, the only other independent pharmacy in town.

"As it turned out, many people preferred to stay with an independent," Addie says. "We stayed open until 7 p.m. and that helped."

From the beginning, the partners decided they wouldn't carry supplies that didn't deal directly deal with health: no newspapers, cameras, knick-knacks and especially no tobacco. The store was the first in town to carry healthcare supplies like braces and walkers, and they had the first blood pressure machine available to the public. They offered personalized service, such as providing information to clients about their prescriptions and keeping patient profiles, long before it was standard practice in pharmacies. They had the region's first diabetes centre, which provided blood glucose meters and diabetes counselling. In 1986, they were the first pharmacy in town to computerize.

Addie became interested in bio-identical hormone replacement after a friend loaned her a book on the subject. She did a lot of research and became a local resource

Adaline and Cathie have always been close. Cathie has followed in her mom's footsteps by becoming a pharmacist and taking over the business Adaline established.

for many women. This lead to the pharmacy compounding (making on site) specialty hormone capsules, suppositories and creams. As well, she explored her interest in alternative therapies, such as herbal medications and specialty vitamins, again before other pharmacies carried or promoted them.

Another new idea came about unintentionally. When the partners noticed people were buying distilled water to drink, they decided to distill their own water instead of paying to ship it into town. When the people heard they had purified water, they wanted to buy it, and the pharmacy was in the water business. They soon switched to reverse osmosis purification, and developed K & H Pure Water as a separate business.

Cathie worked for her mom when she was a teenager but she wasn't particularly interested in pharmacy at the time. After graduating from high school, she "kicked around for awhile" in Vancouver and Victoria but she didn't really know what she wanted to do. She tried a few different things, finally applying to a number of universities for different programs, including agriculture, veterinary and pharmacy. She was accepted into two UBC faculties, and having to make the choice, realized that pharmacy was the place for her. After graduating in 1993 she'd had enough of the city and came home to work for Kornak and Hamm. Addie was pleased, and she hoped, but didn't assume, that Cathie would stay with the company. Cathie made no promises. She and her mother have always gotten along well. "We've always done a lot of laughing," Cathie says, but in terms of the business, there was a certain amount of expectation, and Cathie had no business education or experience.

One day Addie told her "you have to read the stuff on your desk." Cathie didn't have a desk. Addie just smiled and pointed to her own desk, and that's how Cathie became the official manager at age thirty. Addie stayed on as a staff pharmacist, doing what she loved best. She always set the tone by example, and Cathie had always been watching, so as far as the clientele were concerned, it was business as usual.

In the meantime, Harry wanted to retire. They worked out a deal where Cathie bought his share of the pharmacy and he took the water company. He stayed on part-time at the store until health problems forced him to retire in 2000. Addie wanted to work less too, so she cut back to part-time. That gave her time to specialize in hormone counselling and alternative therapies, giving consultations and after-hours sessions. She didn't retire as a practising pharmacist until she was in her late seventies.

Over the years staffing has been an issue. When the USA and Ontario added a year to their pharmacy programs, there was a year with no graduates, which caused quite a shortage of pharmacists. When grocery stores added pharmacies, there was more competition for staff. Pharmacists didn't necessarily want to come to Williams Lake either, so many have come and gone, but luckily some settled in Williams Lake, often because their husbands have jobs in the area. Besides Cathie, the pharmacy employs three part-time pharmacists and seven support staff. The business has physically doubled in size, but the focus on providing solid pharmacy services to its clientele hasn't changed.

When the children were young, the Hamms bought a place on Chimney Lake, and the family spent a lot of time there. Addie was hands-on when it came to building the cabin. She expressed her artistic side by building the fireplace out of local stone. The entire family worked on building the cabin and taking care of the property. The Hamm children are all good cooks because both Addie and Martin were away a fair bit and worked long hours. Martin's job kept him travelling all over the huge school district, and he was away for a time getting his master's degree. Addie was often away taking courses or on council business.

Along with her work and related activities, and raising the four children, Addie was a member of the University Women's Club (UWC), volunteered for UNICEF, and found time to play bridge. She dabbled in the arts, doing well at painting and pottery, and she is an avid supporter of the Station House Gallery. The UWC petered out but she still plays bridge, and finally has time to read. She was nominated for Citizen of the Year in 2003 for her work in assisting with the Lifeline program, setting up pharmacies in Williams Lake and the 100 Mile House hospitals, and her involvement with the Child Development Centre.

Cathie enjoys living in the Cariboo, with its opportunities to mountain bike, skate and cross-country ski. She is a member of the kennel club, largely to keep her border collies entertained, as well as a member of the Williams Lake Studio Theatre and the Central Cariboo Hospice Society. She and her partner, Mary-Jo, enjoy puttering on their lot on Williams Lake.

"The gardens keep getting bigger, as does Mary-Jo's obsession with planting new trees," says Cathie. The couple have three grown children and provide a home to five dogs and seven cats, all rescued animals.

Although they no longer work together, Addie and Cathie see a lot of each other, and have gone on holidays together. And the philosophy at the store hasn't changed—the focus is still on people.

5

POLITICIANS' WIVES

Ruth Fraser

Skiing Keeps Her Young

Ruth Fraser says she hasn't done anything of note. The record says otherwise.

Her husband, Jim, is known as an "over-achiever" in community activities, and along with his volunteer work, he was on Williams Lake Town Council for twelve years, six as mayor. Ruth has always been at his side, and along with an impressive record of her own as a volunteer, she has won two battles with cancer.

Ruth Johansen, the oldest daughter in a family of ten children, grew up on a farm near Domremy, a small community in Saskatchewan. Her parents emigrated from a small island in Norway in the early 1900s, and Ruth didn't speak English until she started school. The farm raised wheat, cattle, chickens and pigs, and even in the midst of the Depression, Ruth says they always had good things to eat. The one-hundred-year-old farm in Saskatchewan is still in the Johansen family, operated by Ruth's brother and his son. The Frasers have been back to visit many times. They have also visited the Norwegian island where Ruth's parents were born.

Ruth received her early education in a one-room school, Grades 1 to 10, all taught by one teacher. When she finished Grade 10, she went to the Pitman Business College in Vancouver, where she stayed with relatives.

Ruth worked for a New Westminster ambulance company until she contracted tuberculosis when she was twenty-five. She spent time in the Heather Pavilion (Vancouver General Hospital) before going home to the farm to recuperate. When she recovered, she worked in a sanitorium in Prince Albert until the Johansens moved to BC so her dad could open a store in the Norwegian community in Matsqui. The Fraser River floods of 1948 hit Matsqui, and the Johansens had to move themselves and the store stock by motorboat to Abbotsford, where they lived in a couple of shacks and sold a few groceries until it was safe to go home.

Jim was living in Vancouver in January 1957 when Ruth met him through a friend on a blind date. They married in August.

Ruth's youngest sister, Sally, and her husband, Dick Chappell, were living in Williams Lake, where Dick had a service station. He suggested Jim join him, and the Frasers came to Williams Lake in 1959. They arrived on December 26 and stayed at the Sunnyside Motel. Ruth remembers having New Year's Dinner at the Lakeview Cafe. The men set up DJ's Sales and Service and Ruth did the books. Jim later established Northside Shell.

In 1960 Finning Tractor built the first large new building in Williams Lake, and Ruth was their first secretary. She went to Vancouver to learn how to operate the teletype. Daughter Colleen joined the family in 1961, and son Scott in 1963. Ruth took time off work and stayed home with them although she still did the books for Jim.

She joined the Cariboo Memorial Hospital Auxiliary in 1966. She is one of the longest-serving members, and an honourary lifetime member. When she first joined the auxiliary, its main fundraiser was an evening of entertainment. It was a huge undertaking, with skits (written by Gwen Ringwood) and musical numbers. Most of the town was involved as participants or audience. Another auxiliary service is the cart, which carries whatever a patient might need or want and is wheeled around the wards every day. Ruth made the rounds with it once when she herself was a recuperating patient.

In the 1960s, there were two stampede queens. Contestants were chosen by ticket sales, and whoever sold the most tickets won. Ruth and Joyce Norberg initiated a different system whereby the contestants had lessons in deportment, makeup, speech and horsemanship, and one winner was chosen by independent judges. They did this for several years before the stampede association took over the contest. This method for the competition has remained.

The Frasers lived on Western Avenue before that area was on sewer, when they just had septic tanks. The airport subdivision was in the process of being developed. Landscaping was a problem because cows from the dairy farm (industrial site now) frequently came calling. In 1965 they built a new house further up the block. That year Jim was elected to the first of his six two-year terms on town council. He was elected mayor in 1971.

It was the custom then for the mayor to entertain visiting dignitaries, such as the prime minister and, once, the entire provincial cabinet. The social events were often held at the Fraser home and Ruth was the official hostess. She frequently accompanied Jim to local events and on official trips. He felt it was his duty to accept all invitations, no matter how big or small, and once they went to six dinners in five days. They also chaperoned the stampede queens on their official travels, such as the Nanaimo Bathtub races, which were something to remember.

Ruth's first cancer struck in 1974. The children were young and it was a difficult time for her, but she says she had great support from friends and neighbours, and she came though it with a clean bill of health. That same year she started the Toastmistress Club and became charter president. Her involvement took her on visits to Quesnel, Kitimat, Prince Rupert and Dawson Creek. Jobs were easy to get in the 1960s to 1980s and Ruth held a number of part-time jobs, but continued to volunteer. She was a director of the Hough Memorial Cancer Society, and in 2002 she joined the Sons of Norway. She is still treasurer of that group.

When Jim left council, he went into real estate. The Frasers built a house at Chimney Lake and moved there in 1982. It was rocky land and Ruth picked hundreds of rocks to clear space. They used the rocks to riprap the shoreline. Ruth said the work really built up her muscles. Through a neighbour at Chimney Lake, she became interested in fitness, an interest she has never lost. In 1985 she started an exercise program at the Williams Lake Seniors' Centre, and led it for twenty years. More recently she's taken the classes to the residents at Glen Arbour, the city's in-town seniors' residence. "I help them and they help me," Ruth says. The sessions are mini-social affairs with refreshments served after the exercises.

Then there is skiing. The Frasers started skiing at the Squaw Valley ski hill when the children were young, and continued enjoying the sport when Mount Timothy Ski Hill was built. Jim was sixty-five when he took the instructor's course, and Ruth took the course when she was sixty-nine. "I thought I knew how to ski, but that course taught me differently," she says, adding "it's a great sport for older people."

They both had ski students of all ages, and Ruth's oldest student was seventy-one. They were at the hill at least

Ruth Fraser says skiing keeps her young. She and husband Jim took up the sport when their children were small and stayed with it, both becoming instructors when they were in their sixties. Ruth says it's a great sport for older people.

twice a week for years, either instructing students or skiing themselves. In 2009, after a few warning spells on the ski hill, Ruth had a pacemaker installed, and was soon back in action.

She and Jim were on their way to Mount Timothy in January 2011 when they were involved in a motor vehicle accident. Both were seriously injured, Ruth with multiple fractures. It was during her time in the hospital that the second cancer was discovered behind her pacemaker. In the fall she underwent two operations to deal with that. What with the exercising and skiing, Ruth is in excellent physical shape, and the doctors said she might not have survived the accident if she hadn't been.

Ruth would rather talk about skiing than the difficulties. She and Jim went to the ski hill for a visit as soon as they were discharged from the hospital after the accident, not to ski, but because they have such good memories there. She says you don't have to ski to enjoy Mount Timothy. For a number of years she's organized a Valentine's Day trip to the hill for seniors. They go by bus and have lunch. Ruth gives each participant a small gift. The seniors enjoy seeing what "real snow" looks like again and watching skiers in action.

By spring 2012, Ruth was driving again, doing the exercises again and she has every intention of getting back on the ski hill when winter comes.

Susan Zirnhelt

Teacher, Rancher, Politician's Wife

Susan Shaw was a city girl, born and raised in Vancouver where her father was a newspaperman. She was attending the University of British Columbia when she met David Zirnhelt. She was the education representative on the Alma Mater Society (student council), and David was the group's president.

David was born and raised in the Cariboo, in the 150 Mile House area. In 1969 he ran as the Liberal candidate in the provincial election against the Social Credit's Alex Fraser. Fraser won. Susan and David were married in 1971, and went to Ottawa when David was seconded to work as an executive assistant in the Ministry of State for Urban Affairs. He and Susan rented a small farm, which was David's idea, the first year they were there, but the difficulty of travelling on winter roads convinced them to move into the city. Susan taught French in kindergarten to Grade 6 in an Ottawa school. After two years in Ottawa, they returned to BC.

David worked as regional director for Opportunities for Youth for BC and Yukon, but his heart was set on ranching in the Cariboo. "We tried a couple of angles that didn't work out, and we finally bought seventy-four acres from David's dad in the Beaver Valley," Susan says.

The property was beside Chambers Lake and it is a beautiful spot, but it had a few shortcomings. There was no road access for one thing, and they had to leave their vehicle on the other side of the lake and cross by boat. There was no house either. David and Susan planted a big garden in the spring of 1974, and moved to the ranch to stay that summer when son Damon was seven months old. They lived in a tent, with Susan cooking on a campfire, while they built a cabin. The garden did well, and by September there was a bumper crop of tomatoes. Susan canned them over the campfire.

They didn't get the cabin finished until November, and it didn't have any conveniences. There was a wood stove and no plumbing. They not only carried water, but in the winter they had to chop a hole through the ice in the lake to get it. "I didn't try to wash many clothes," Susan says. "We took the laundry to the laundromat.

Son Sam was born before they had a road, and Susan and David made the first part of the trip to the hospital boating across the lake at night. The truck broke down at Big Lake and they had to wake people up to get a ride to town.

Developing a ranch from scratch, as it were, takes a lot of hard work and it isn't a speedy process. It was three years before they had a road, and then it was what Susan calls a challenge road, in that it challenged every vehicle. It was ten kilometres to connect to the Likely Road and Susan carried a saw, axe, shovel and coveralls with her in case she got stuck, which she frequently did. It was nine years before they had a bridge across the creek and a real road out to the main road.

Susan Zirnhelt says she isn't really a horse person, preferring smaller animals, but one learns all kinds of skills on a ranch out of necessity. The Zirnhelts used horses for ranch work, so Susan learned to handle a team.

Then there was the question of having an income while getting the ranch established. It was practical for Susan to be the earner while David did the ranch work, so he looked after the boys while she went back to the classroom. She substituted at Big Lake Elementary, then taught part-time in Williams Lake, first at Crescent Heights and later Nesika and the 150 Mile.

The trip to Williams Lake from the ranch had its moments. "We only had a decrepit old vehicle and some of the teachers were astonished that I could keep it going," Susan recalls. She isn't mechanical but she learned a few tricks. David started a consulting business in land use and planning and they lived at 150 Mile for a time when she was teaching at Nesika and he was working with the Canim Lake Band. Susan's parents stayed at the ranch. "My sixty-year-old mother looked after the chickens and learned to milk the cow," she says. "We'd go home on weekends to haul hay."

Susan and David were still in the pioneering stage of establishing their ranch when sons Damon and Sam were little.

Susan stayed home when Damon was in Grade 1. David's consulting work kept him away a fair bit, and she didn't mind being on her own. She's always had a dog, usually a border collie, but she kept an ear out for strange noises. They acquired more property as they could, and along with cattle, David raised and trained draft horses. Susan says she isn't really a horse person. "I can drive a team," she says, "but I'm more into small animals and the garden."

She's always had a large garden. They also have a wood lot and David practised sustainable logging using horses.

Susan went back to teaching full-time in 1983. She taught at rural schools, first at Big Lake Elementary, then at Likely, from kindergarten to Grade 10. When Robin, the youngest son, started school he went with her. She taught a Grade 4/5/6 split, and French to the junior high grades. She taught at Likely for twenty-two years. She loved teaching, but getting to school could be an adventure.

It's a forty-seven-kilometre drive from the Zirnhelt ranch to the Likely school, and in winter the trip was no joy. For the first few years the road wasn't paved and there were dozens of logging trucks travelling on it. Susan had a small car and she was sometimes run off the road by the big rigs. Few truckers stopped to see if she got going again. She only missed one day of school and that was because the road was closed.

She had some close calls, including a run-in with a moose, but one morning, on an icy road in the freezing rain, she had the fright of her life. Robin was with her, and she came over the crest of a hill to see a logging truck sideways at the bottom. It was completely blocking the road. She managed to stop, but to her horror another truck came over the hill behind her. It was a heart-stopping moment, but the driver of the second truck had his wits about him and drove off the road.

In 1975 David took his first step back into politics when he was elected as a director on the Cariboo Regional District. He later switched to the District #27 school board and served as chair. In 1989 he ran as the New Democratic Party (NDP) candidate for the Cariboo in a by-election and won. Ironically, the seat was vacant because of the death of the incumbent, Alex Fraser.

Susan had been involved in the 1969 election, and she helped again in 1989, mostly by selling memberships, but after that, except for supporting him and taking a turn working in the campaign office during elections, she stayed in the background. David was away from home even more often during the twelve years he was in provincial government, and Susan and the boys kept the home fires burning. Their ranching partner looked after the cattle, and they got rid of the milk cow, but otherwise it was business as usual on the ranch, the boys continued their education and Susan continued to enjoy her teaching career.

It was not always business as usual in their personal lives. David was the first NDP MLA in the history of the Cariboo, and although he was elected three times, many Cariboo people don't like the NDP. He had a high profile right from the start as he began with a cabinet appointment, and he held a number of cabinet posts, including Minister of Forests. Some of his constituents had expectations he had no way to meet. At times people expressed their disappointment unpleasantly and the boys came in for their share of it. There were some ugly incidents, complaints and accusations that Susan prefers not to dwell on.

Robin was six when his dad was elected MLA. Once when David came home after a longer than usual absence, he was met with a notice attached to the front door. It was from Robin. It said, "Wanted, MLA David Zirnhelt, For Abandoning 10 year old son." That was a tough one, but David's time in office certainly wasn't all downers.

"On a positive note, the family had a wonderful opportunity to learn about government and to develop an understanding of the role of citizens in a democracy," Susan says. "We also had occasion to meet many wonderful people during their dad's tenure."

As a cabinet minister David did some travelling overseas, but because she was teaching full-time, Susan didn't get to go with him, except for a trip to Spain in the summer of 1992. "David was Minister of Small Business and Trade and went to officiate for BC Day Celebrations at Expo '92, and we stayed over for a few days," Susan says, adding that at the time, "spouses had to pay their own way"

For years the Zirnhelts have held sleigh-ride parties with a bonfire every winter for their neighbours, and for years after David was elected they hosted a summer weekend camp-out and barbecue on the ranch. This was a huge event with people coming from all ends of the constituency to attend. There were many helping hands but it took a lot of organizing and energy on Susan's part to pull it together. The event did trigger a rumour that was funny under the circumstances. The word got around that David wouldn't let any campers in his house to use the bathroom facilities, they had to use the outhouse. The truth was that the biffy was the Zirnhelt's bathroom facility. The house was too close to the lake to have a septic field. Susan didn't get her dream house, a beautiful log home complete with a sewing room and indoor plumbing, until the late 1990s.

David lost his seat in the 2001 election but he didn't lose his interest in politics. He has remained active in the NDP and he serves on the boards of a number of non-profit organizations. He still does a fair amount of travelling. Susan retired from teaching in 2007 and she and David are focusing on organic farming. They belong to a group of ranchers called "Healthy Steppes" who collaborate in promoting grass-fed beef. They also hold on-ranch apprenticeships in grass-fed ranching. Susan continues to grow a big garden and keep small animals. She also has some small people to enjoy, three grandsons and one granddaughter. Sons Damon and Sam and their families live on the ranch where they operate Zirnhelt Timber Frames.

Lynnette Cobb

You Just Do What You Have To Do

*T*hat dark-haired lady with a smile on her face you often see whipping around Williams Lake streets in a motorized wheelchair is Lynnette Cobb. She is probably on her way to help someone.

Lynnette hasn't always smiled about being in a wheelchair. She says her first public appearance on wheels was devastating. She adds, "there are only two ways to deal with adversity: give up or fight back." She's been fighting back against multiple sclerosis since 1982. She says being a "stubborn Swede" has seen her through.

Lynnette is married to Walter Cobb, who served the people of Williams Lake for sixteen years on city council, six as mayor, and then a term as the Cariboo South MLA. He has a high profile in the community as a long-time member of the Chamber of Commerce and other organizations. Lynnette may not make the headlines, but she makes her own contributions to the community.

The Cobbs have always worked as a team. Whatever Walt undertakes, Lynnette is there beside him, and he supports her endeavours. This approach has worked well for almost half a century, through good times and some not-so-good times. The not-so good times include Lynnette's MS.

Lynnette spent her early years in Chilliwack where her father, Sven Swanson, had a dairy farm. Lynnette was the baby of the family, with two older brothers.

"I was pretty spoiled," she says, but she grew up in a hurry when her mother died after a long illness. There was no medicare then. The bills were costly, so times weren't easy. After her mother's death in 1957, the family moved to the Cariboo to the Big Lake Ranch.

Lynnette remembers the move as exciting. She'd always had a horse. She learned to ride about the time she learned to walk, and at Big Lake she got to ride to school. She helped with the ranch work and was chief cook and bottle washer for her dad and brothers. She went to town for Grade 9, staying at the student dormitory. She says it was a positive experience. "The matron, Mrs. Whitmore, was like a mother, a strict but caring mother," she says. The students, both boys and girls, took turns doing the chores, but there was always time for fun.

Lynnette Cobb has always had a love for horses. She began riding as a youngster and continued for as long as she could before MS put her in a wheelchair.

In Grade 11, Lynnette ran for stampede queen, but she didn't make it. "I didn't know the proper way to ride," she says. "I just got on a horse and rode. That worked for chasing cattle through the bush but not so much for stampede queen."

When it came time for the graduation party Lynnette had no way to get to it. The dorm kids didn't have much social interaction with the other students, but she had seen Walt around, and he had a vehicle, so she asked him to be her date for the party. He accepted. That was on June 4, 1965. They became engaged on June 21 and were married September 11. "People kept looking at me to see if I was pregnant, but I wasn't," Lynnette recalls with a laugh.

Walt's parents gave them a cabin in Pine Valley, and they added on to it. Both were working at SuperValu (in Mackenzie's Store) but the management wasn't keen on a married couple working together, so Lynnette went to work for Carson Truck Lines. When Mackenzie's owner, Doug Stevenson, heard about this he said it was a silly rule and Lynnette went back to SuperValu.

Walt later worked for Lord's Men's Wear, and when it sold, he and Lynnette decided to go into business themselves. They opened Walt's Men's Shop in 1969. That same year, they adopted son Randy, and in 1972, daughter Toni. Lynnette stayed home with the children for a time, but she kept books for Hugo Stahl of Sportsman's Esso.

Then she opened Lynnette's Look, a ladies' wear shop, in the Hodgson Place Mall beside Walt's shop. They later bought a building on Oliver Street and moved both businesses there. Lynnette says when they went on business trips, suppliers sometimes called her Mrs. Walt, but there were times when they called Walt Mr. Lynnette.

The Cobbs moved from Pine Valley to "town" in the fall of 1973. They lived at Odine's trailer court while Walt built a house on 12th Avenue. He was elected to city council in 1980, and was one of the few Williams Lake mayors to serve more than one term.

Lynnette's first inkling that something was amiss was feeling numbness in her feet. In 1982 she was diagnosed with MS. The news was shocking. It progressed slowly, but the time came when she had to sell the shop. That was extremely hard to deal with. "I really enjoyed the shop, especially meeting people," she says, "but you just have to do what you have to do. "

In 1985 the Cobbs moved to acreage at the 150 Mile. They'd always had horses, and at one time they had five. They kept them at Big Lake while her dad had the ranch, then at a ranch on Fox Mountain. Randy and Toni had their own horses and they all did a lot of riding. At 150 Mile the horses were handy. Lynnette rode as long

Lynnette and husband, Walter, shared smiles and a hug when he was elected mayor of Williams Lake in 1990. Lynnette was a politician's wife for quite some time. Walt began his sixteen-year stint on council when he was elected an alderman in 1980. He later served a term as a Liberal MLA.

as she could. Horses had been such a big part of her life, it was a crushing blow when she had to give up riding. "The horses knew when I had a problem, they'd just stand there. Even when I couldn't ride any more, I could go and talk to them," she says.

Old horses always got special treatment. The Cobbs couldn't bear to sell them, and all but one died of old age. After they moved back to town the horses were boarded out again. The last one was retired in 2006. Lynnette said they always had good horses and she's been blessed with her family who always supported her love of them.

Lynnette's dad died in 1991. His death left a big void in her life; they had been very close. "He'd been my mom as well as my dad for so many years," she explains.

She felt she had to do something, and that something was taking training and working for the Canadian Mental Health Association's Crisis Line. The work included crisis intervention and supportive counselling on a twenty-four-hour basis with volunteers manning the phones. Lynnette now does similar work for the RCMP's Victim Services Program. This justice-related service gives emotional support and encouragement to victims of crime, helping them understand how the system works and supporting them through the process. Both the Crisis Line and Victim Services require caring, compassionate counsellors, and Lynnette fits the bill.

"Sometimes people just need someone to talk to, someone to listen, someone to care," she says. In 1997 she was chosen Citizen of the Year for over fifty-thousand hours of volunteer work. Both Cobbs were involved in establishing Baker Manor, a home for the physically handicapped in Williams Lake. Lynnette organized an MS Self-Help Group where people can get together and compare notes.

Walt was elected MLA in 2001, and he was often in Victoria for weeks on end. He bought a park unit in a beautiful site in Victoria and moved their motorhome there so Lynnette and the dog could be with him. He would be gone from seven in the morning until nine at night. "He doesn't do anything halfway," Lynnette notes.

Once when asked what it was like being married to a celebrity, Lynnette made a rather pithy comment indicating Walt was the same person he'd always been. He says she's very effective in keeping him in line. "No one belongs on a pedestal," she says with a grin.

The Cobbs moved back to town in 1997 when Lynnette was no longer able to drive. Their present home overlooks the stampede grounds, just a few blocks from downtown. And it has a spectacular view of the lake. Along with horses Lynnette has always had a dog, and her current one is named Gus. He came from the SPCA and is her constant companion and guardian.

In March 2011, Lynnette went to a clinic in California for what some consider to be a controversial treatment for MS. While she won't walk again, she is happy with the results. "For the first time in years I can feel my feet and wear shoes," she says.

In the summer of 2011, Walt announced he was going to run for mayor. As it happened, another former mayor also entered the race against the incumbent. The incumbent won. Life will go on for the Cobbs, and neither is likely to stop their work in the community. Both Randy and Toni live in the city, and Lynnette and Walt enjoy spending time with the seven grandchildren. They enjoy travelling too, and have covered a lot of country in the motorhome.

Sheila Wyse

Charlie's Wife, and So Much More

When she introduces herself to people, Sheila Wyse is often greeted with, "Oh, you're Charlie's wife."

She is. Husband Charlie is a well-known retired teacher and Cariboo politician. He taught for thirty-five years at Columneetza and Williams Lake Secondary schools. He was a city councillor for twenty-three years and Cariboo Chilcotin MLA for one term. As this is written he is the NDP candidate for the next provincial election.

Sheila has a long list of accomplishments of her own. They include ten years' service with the Cariboo Chilcotin Teachers' Association, including three years as president, and serving as a volunteer with numerous community organizations.

Sheila was raised in Vancouver but met Charlie at St. Ann's Academy when her family moved to Kamloops. The two kept in touch when Charlie went to UBC to get his teacher's degree. They married after Sheila's high school graduation while Charlie was still at university. They had two children, Charles, born in 1966, and Anne-Marie, who arrived in 1968.

In 1969 the family moved to Williams Lake where Charlie had accepted a job at Columneetza Secondary. Sheila was a stay-at-home mom during their early years in the community. She was actively involved in many of the children's activities as well as community events. She led storytime at the city's library when it was attached to city hall and chaired the Central Cariboo Music and Drama Festival for three years. She volunteered at Cataline Elementary where her children attended school. One day, the principal asked her to fill in for a teacher who had gone home sick. In the 1970s, certified teachers were in short supply, particularly in rural areas. Sheila began to fill in when certified teachers were unavailable. "Sometimes it was more like babysitting," she recalls. "The school needed an adult in the room and were happy to have anyone to do the job."

These opportunities led Sheila to begin working on her teaching degree. She took courses at Cariboo College in Williams Lake, through summer school at UBC, and through UBC's Distance Learning Program. After almost ten years of this routine she received an ultimatum from UBC saying she had to complete her degree within ten years from the start of her program or begin all over again. So, with Charles in a nursing program at Vancouver General Hospital, and Anne-Marie entering Grade 12 at Columneetza, Sheila went to UBC as a full-time student in elementary education. She did a practicum at Glendale Elementary and planned to complete her final year at summer school, but in July she learned she had a scholarship as the top student in primary education that year. The money could only be used for a winter session, so in September she headed back to UBC to complete her final year. In June 1985 the whole family attended Sheila's graduation.

"I wasn't missing that event," said Sheila. "I'd worked ten years to get that degree and I was going to celebrate." At the ceremony in UBC's War Memorial Gym, the family watched as Sheila crossed the stage to receive her graduation scroll. Just as the Chancellor tapped her on the head (a tradition at UBC commencement ceremonies) son Charles called out, in a voice that filled the huge room, "Way to go, Mom!"

Over the next twenty years Sheila taught at most of the elementary schools in the Williams Lake area. Soon after she began teaching she became active in the Cariboo Chilcotin Teachers' Association. "I saw there was a job to be done and I thought it was important and I had time to do it," she explains.

She initially worked in union positions at the school level at various times as staff rep, health and safety rep, or as professional development rep. She also served as vice-president for a year before being elected president. She served as president for three years. She enjoyed the job but in the fall of 2005 BC teachers went on a full strike, withdrawing services and walking a picket line, and she hadn't expected that.

"There was a lot of angst among teachers," Sheila recalls. "Few teachers had ever been involved in a full strike and it was difficult for them, but they were fighting for better conditions for their students."

Both the Wyse children got married in the mid-nineties and grandson Clayton was born in 1997. In 1998, tragedy struck when son Charles succumbed to leukemia. He had been diagnosed with the disease in 1996 while working as a critical care nurse at Vancouver General Hospital. His initial treatment was successful and he returned to work, but he suffered a relapse and died in May.

Sheila retired from teaching in 2007 and since then she has been actively involved with community groups. They include serving on the Station House Gallery Board, Cariboo Chilcotin Retired Teachers' Association, Elder College Curriculum Committee, Cariboo Festival, the Williams Lake Seniors' Advisory Committee, and the local chapter of the Council of Canadians. She was a founding director of the Central Cariboo Arts and Culture Society, serving first on their working committee and then as a director for one year. As this story is written she is serving her third term as chair of the society that operates the Museum of the Cariboo Chilcotin. She has also worked as a facilitator for the Roots of Empathy program. This involves working with a class of students and a volunteer mother and her baby. The mom and baby visit with the students each month during the school year as the children observe the baby's growth and development.

Sheila and Charlie have done some travelling, mostly personal holiday time during summer vacations, but they had an opportunity to go to Nigeria when Charlie served as MLA. He represented the Opposition at the Commonwealth Conference in 2006 in Abuja, the capital of Nigeria.

"He was told he could have one first-class ticket or two tourist-class tickets, and then I could go too," Sheila remembers. "Lucky for him he chose the latter option."

Sheila Wyse has been active in the community for many years, especially since she retired from teaching. As this is written she is, among other things, president of the Williams Lake Museum and Historical Society, which operates the Museum of the Cariboo Chilcotin.

The Wyse family arrived in Williams Lake in 1969 when Charlie accepted a teaching position with School District #27. They are pictured here with son Charles and daughter Anne-Marie. Charlie was on city council for twenty-three years, MLA for one term, and is currently the NDP candidate for the next provincial election.

It was an eye-opening adventure as Nigeria is not a country on the list of recommended vacation spots.

Sheila is an avid gardener and belongs to the local garden club. She also likes to play with fabric, and loves to quilt. "It just seems there aren't enough hours to do all the things I enjoy," she says. Both she and Charlie are walkers and they often leave their car in the driveway to walk to town. She's handy around the house too, explaining she's always been interested in doing what used to be called "boy stuff."

"Now I prefer to use that time in my sewing room," she says.

Her latest interest is playing the ukulele with a group that meets on Wednesdays at the arts centre. "It's a great way to learn something new and enjoy the pleasure of singing together in a group."

Sheila and Charlie spend as much time as they can with Anne-Marie and grandson Clayton, who live in Wetaskiwin, Alberta. Anne-Marie's family has expanded to include partner Dave and his daughter, Jennifer.

"Jenn and I enjoy quilting together while Clayton and I enjoy listening to our collection of vinyl records," Sheila says.

When asked about the future Sheila says Williams Lake is home. "While we only intended to stay for a year or two when we came, we have been very happy here. Each time I go away I'm always happy to come back home. It's been a great place to raise a family and a wonderfully supportive community for Charlie and me."

Charanjit Rathor

She Keeps the Home Fires Burning

By the end of his current term in office, Charanjit Rathor's husband, Surinderpal, will be the longest-ever member of Williams Lake City Council. He will have served twenty-four years. For the last twenty-one years, Charan has been managing the home, leaving him free to do his duties on council and to participate in community activities. Surinder, who is an electrician with Tolko Industries (a forest company), has received numerous awards for his many services to the community.

Charan came to BC from India when she was eleven years old, with her parents, Kishan Singh and Baldev Kaur Parmar, her older sister, Parmajit, and younger brother Surinder. The family lived in the Punjab state when Kishan was in the army, and later in Delhi, where he was with the Indian Post and Telegraph Department. Mrs. Parmar had relatives in BC who sent home good reports of the province, so they decided to immigrate. They arrived in 1969 and stayed with Mrs. Parmar's brother in Nanaimo before coming to Williams Lake. At the time most of the South Asian newcomers lived in the Glendale community, and Charan, who didn't speak English, was one of the many Sikh children who came under the wing of Glendale school principal Hazel Huckvale.

Kishan went to work at the Pinette and Therrien Mill and he was soon a moving force in the Canadian Punjabi Committee, a group that was formed to help the South Asian newcomers adjust to Western culture. The group raised money to build

Born in India, raised in Williams Lake, Charanjit Rathor has kept her traditional Sikh culture while embracing Western ways.

the Guru Nanak Sikh Temple, and Kishan was also involved in working with the general community. Because of her dad's involvement, Charan grew up with an awareness of community events.

When she finished school, Charan went to work at the Bil Nor restaurant, first as a dishwasher, and then as cook. She worked at numerous local restaurants until her marriage in 1975. The marriage was arranged by her sister Parmi and Parmi's husband, Harbhajan Parhar. Harbhajan knew Surinderpal in India.

Charan, an accomplished cook of both South Asian and Western cuisine, cooks up a storm in her kitchen with friend Charanjit Grewal.

The Rathors have two children, Robin, who lives in Vancouver with his wife and family, and daughter Roop, who lives with her husband and three children in Williams Lake.

When the children were older Charan resumed her work as a cook, and she was at Cariboo Lodge seniors' care facility when it closed, but her focus has always been on the family. She not only looks after the personal family affairs, she also looks after the extended family, as both her parents and Surinderpal's parents live in Williams Lake. Although Charan has health problems herself, when anyone in the family is ill or recuperating, she is the caregiver. She also spends as much time as she can with Roop's three children, Pria, Ria and Digraj, who live nearby.

She knits, is an excellent seamstress, and of course an excellent cook, whether it be entertaining at home or cooking for events at the temple. She also grows a huge garden.

She and Surinderpal like to travel but Charan also travels on her own.

She has gone with friends or family to New York and Montreal and has taken numerous trips to India.

The Rathors have an apartment in India where they stay on their visits there.

Except for entertaining guests (she is a charming hostess) and accompanying Surinderpal to some events, Charan plays no part in Surinderpal's political life.

"I don't like politics," she explains with a smile, "so I look after all the other things,"

"And I couldn't do what I do without her," Surinder says.

Tammy French

Time to Smell the Roses

Tammy French was assistant to Forest Minister David Zirnhelt in the early 1990s. Her husband, Paul, was a city councillor at the time, and there were so many topics that were out of bounds because of confidentiality the only conversation the couple could safely have was about their family.

Tammy was born in Revelstoke where her dad, Larry Winters, worked for the CPR. In 1964 the family moved to 100 Mile House. Tammy, who is the third of the seven Winters' children, attended school there. In 1978, the family moved to Williams Lake and she joined them after graduating from Peter Skene Ogden. She was working at the Dog Patch in Williams Lake when she met Paul, and they were married in 1980.

Tammy was a stay-at-home mom with Allen, Michelle and Jenni. Both Tammy and Paul were active ballplayers, playing fun ball, slo-pitch and orthodox. At one point they played in three different leagues at the same time: 150 Mile, Chilcotin and Wildwood. As soon as the children were old enough to hold a bat, they were playing ball too. Allen knew all the words to "Take Me Out to the Ball Game" when he was three. When Tammy wasn't playing ball or keeping score for some team or another, she was coaching kids' teams.

When Jenni started school, Tammy went to work at a corner store, the HandiMart. In 1993, Paul ran for city council. It was a family affair, with Tammy going door-knocking with him as well as helping behind the scenes and the kids helping distribute brochures, but once elected, she left the politics to him. Later that year, she went to work in Zirnhelt's office as constituency assistant. This was an entirely new world for her. She was used to working with people

Tammy French with her oldest daughter, Michelle Weir, (left) and Jenni Hoyer, her youngest daughter (right). Tammy and her husband, Paul, also have one son.

and meeting the public, but she knew nothing about politics or how the provincial government worked. David's ministerial assistant, Wendy McPhee, and Tammy had gone to school together in 100 Mile, so that was a plus.

Because David was forest minister in a forestry town, the office was a busy one. Tammy recalls going to a meeting when she first started the job to take minutes. David was discussing local forest issues with local lumbermen. "I didn't know what they were talking about, so I wrote down everything," she says.

She learned quickly. The office dealt with people who had all kinds of problems but what upset her were the social service issues. "I had no idea so many people had problems or how many problems there were for them to have," she says. "It certainly opened my eyes."

There were some unforgettable moments. Once she'd driven David to 100 Mile House for a meeting. He was going on to Victoria, and when it started snowing he told her to head home. She waited too long, and the highway was treacherous with blowing snow. She drove into the first pullout and phoned Paul to tell him she was too frightened to go any further. He told her to try and get to a restaurant at Lac La Hache and he'd come and get her. They left the car there, and Tammy says she still gets white knuckles when she thinks about it.

Tammy was on her own in the office during the 1996 election as Wendy was a political appointee and unemployed once the writ was dropped. Tammy says that was another experience, but David won the election and everything went back to normal.

When Lo's Florists owner, Gillian MacDonald, died in 1997, Tammy and Wendy told Gillian's husband, Brian, that if he ever wanted to sell the business, they'd buy it. They didn't give it another thought until he called one day the next year and said he wanted to sell as soon as possible. Tammy gave her notice first.

Neither she nor Wendy knew anything about flowers or running a business. They didn't know about letters of credit, and by the time they applied, Wendy had left her job and they couldn't get any credit. "After working for the government and knowing how to get help for people, we didn't even think to get any help for ourselves," Tammy says. "We did everything the hard way."

What they did have was an experienced staff and the shop had some loyal customers. The partners thought they were doing okay until they went to Chilliwack late that fall in a pickup truck with a canopy to get a large order of plants and flowers. On the way home an accident in the Fraser Canyon held them up for hours and everything in the canopy froze.

They persevered and the business was going well when Wendy was injured in a car accident and could no longer work. Tammy is now the sole proprietor. She has two full-time staff. Florist Marlene Lamash has been with Lo's for over twenty years, and Laura Unrau joined the staff more recently. At busy times the entire family pitches in to help with deliveries and the grunt work (i.e. de-leafing stems). Occasionally Tammy's grandchildren get into the act as well.

For most of the time Paul was on council, Tammy rarely got to travel with him and sometimes she didn't even get to go to the city's Christmas party. "My work

Lo's Florists is sometimes a three-generation operation. Learning about flowers from Grandma are Hailey and Levi Weir.

at the MLA's office often conflicted, and then the interesting events happened when it was the busy time at the florists," she explains.

Paul was on council for fifteen years. He ran for mayor in 2009 but didn't make it, and he is now president of the local United Steelworkers union. He and Tammy work in the same building and sometimes they can get together for lunch.

"It is rewarding to bring some beauty into people's lives."

Along with playing ball, Paul and Tammy have always been campers. For some years they've parked their trailer at a lake and have escaped to it for at least one day a weekend. Their children are married and all three live in Williams Lake. They too are campers and ballplayers. Tammy and Paul don't travel too far afield, mostly just in BC and Alberta, but when youngest daughter Jenni chose to be married in Las Vegas, they did get there.

While Tammy enjoyed her involvement in political life, she finds life with flowers less stressful and it is rewarding to "bring some beauty" into people's lives.

Back row: Beth Walton, Gaeil Farrar, Anne Blake, Erin Hitchcock, Mary Langstrom.
Front row: Lisa Bowering, Lorie Williston, Gaylene Desaultels. Photo by Monica Lamb-Yorski.

6

THE LADIES OF THE TRIBUNE

Author's note

The staff at the *Williams Lake Tribune* is unique in that with one exception, the editorial staff, the sales staff, front office and production people are all women. The only male is Greg Sabatino, the sports editor, who manages to hold his own very well.

Lorie Williston

President, Interior North, Black Press

Lorie Williston believes success is being passionate about your job no matter what it is.

Williams Lake is Lorie's home base, but her job as president of Interior North Black Press takes her from Ashcroft to Prince Rupert, overseeing the operational functions, editorial, accounting and distribution for the sixteen interior publications in the newspaper chain. She says she's the "bean counter." The job means a lot of time spent on the road as direct air transportation between the communities is all but non-existent.

Lorie came to Williams Lake from Chilliwack in the early 1970s when she was in Grade 6. Williams Lake was booming with the coming of Gibraltar Mines, and her dad, Gordon Cheek, was with Irwin Homes. Gordon had horses when he was young, and always dreamed of having them again. This dream came true in Williams Lake and when his company offered him a job in Prince George, rather than leave Williams Lake and the horses, he left the company and started his own.

Lorie had her own horse, and her interest in riding was one reason she entered the Stampede Queen contest in 1977. She says the training she received and her experiences as queen have served her well in her working career. "The first time I had to speak to a group I was nervous," she says, "but the Toastmistress training all comes back."

Lorie and Mike Williston were high-school sweethearts and they married shortly after Lorie graduated from Columneetza. She worked for a time for the Ministry of Highways' Paving branch, but left after the birth of son Lee because the long hours in paving season didn't leave her time with the baby. Shortly after second son Kyle was born, Mike's mother, Sharon Williston, who worked in the *Tribune*'s accounting department, asked her to help with a publication. One thing led to another, and Lorie went from entry clerk to assistant accounting, then to payroll comptroller, then publisher in 2001. "Being both comptroller and publisher was a bit much," she says.

The nature of her work at the *Tribune* has always meant flexible hours, so she was able to balance family and work. She managed to spend the weekends at the arena when the boys were playing hockey. "I often took my work to the dressing room," she says. "Once I even had T4 slips all over the place, but I was there."

While she has learned on the job, Lorie has taken managerial training through college courses as well. Her message to women is that you can have a career and family, but it is a lot of work, and family has to come first. The trick, she says, is not to get too tied up. The boys were older by the time she had a significant management job so they were okay. "I wouldn't have gone on with my career if they hadn't been," she says.

Mike, who is an equipment operator at Gibraltar, was always supportive, but he drew the line when she was both comptroller and publisher. She'd start at 7 a.m. and often wouldn't get home until 2 a.m. the next morning. Mike put her on a midnight curfew.

"I'm a control freak and I didn't want to give up the comptroller's job. It probably would have been less stressful if I had a degree in business administration," she says.

When David Black separated the Black Press newspaper chain into northern and southern divisions, Lorie became vice-president, and then president, of Interior North. She says she learned from the senior people at the papers, and now they are retiring. Fresh young publishers are coming up and they are going through the learning process.

When the newspaper chain was smaller, it was like a tightly knit family. It's not so much now, Lorie says, but small or big, it still takes teamwork. She always has enjoyed the camaraderie with the people and the challenges of the job. I never know what the day is going to bring," she says.

Lorie has had opportunities to move within the company to other locations, but she has everything she wants in Williams Lake, and her family is there, including both sons and their wives and children. Lee is with provincial fisheries, and Kyle a trucker. She loves the water, and in summer she spends as much time as she can on it or in it. She also enjoys playing golf, but her main focus in her free time is being grandma to two grandchildren.

Beth Walton

Of all the *Tribune* staff, Beth Walton is probably best known by many members of the public. She's been the receptionist for twenty-five years, and she's the one who greets people at the door. She says that's the best part of the job. "I get to know the regular customers on a first-name basis, and there is always someone new coming in," she says.

Along with taking subscriptions and classified ads (she helps with the latter if requested) she directs traffic. If you want to see a staff person, she takes care of that and she's the front line to answer questions.

The Waltons came to Williams Lake in the early 1970s, during the town's big growing spurt. Beth stayed at home with their three children until the youngest was nine, then she took part in a government sponsored re-entry program designed to help women get back into the workforce. The government subsidized wages for six months while the women were trained. The *Tribune* was part of the program, and for no particular reason, Beth sent her resume to the newspaper. She got the training position, and when the six months was over, the job was hers.

Off the job, and actually on the job too, Beth is known for her baking. The *Tribune* staff are among those who appreciate her talents in this department as she frequently brings goodies to work to share with them.

Two of the Walton children still live in Williams Lake, and Beth has three grandchildren there as well.

Lisa Bowering

*T*he *Tribune* team leader is Lisa Bowering. She started with the newspaper as a sales consultant in August 2002. In May 2011, she took on the dual role as publisher and sales manager. She says that unlike most jobs, newspaper work happens when it happens, not necessarily between nine to five.

"No two days are ever the same," she says. "I'll have my daytimer all set when I go home, but when I come in the next morning the phone rings, something will have come up and the plans go out the window."

Lisa was born in Prince Rupert, but moved to the Lower Mainland as a child. Her dad was a commercial fisherman and her mom was in banking. During her school years she was active in sports, and she was a competitive figure skater until she was in Grade 12.

"My mother designed and made all my costumes, and she had to be innovative because she worked with remnants or whatever material she had," Lisa says, "but by the time I hit Grade 12 I was tired of getting up at 4 a.m. to get to practices, and I was more aware of the politics involved in figure skating, so I gave it up." She went into competitive trampoline and rugby.

After her graduation from Richmond Secondary, she worked for a title search company in Vancouver. She met her husband Dave through friends. After the children, Alyx and Patrick, arrived, it became obvious two salaries were needed to live decently in the city, so she went back to work at the title search company, handling client relations and sales.

Dave worked in Vancouver at St. Paul's Hospital for many years, then at Chrysler of Canada's head office. After Lisa returned to work, he and Lisa thought about a change in location. Dave checked the board at the union office one day and spotted an opening for an engineer at Cariboo Memorial Hospital (CMH). That sounded promising, so he applied for the job and got it. The family moved to Williams Lake in November 1989. Since 2000, Dave has been the chief engineer at CMH.

The Bowerings first rented a house in the city, but then decided if they were living in a rural area, they might as well lead the country life. They bought a place at Springhouse where they had chickens and pigs, and sometimes steers. Alyx and

Patrick went to Chimney Lake School. They were at Springhouse for thirteen years before moving back to town.

It didn't take Lisa long to get involved in sports. Columneetza was starting a girls' rugby team, and she coached the first season with Grade 11 and 12 girls (in 1999 it became Grades 8 to 12). They travelled to all the zone matches, and made it to the provincial finals, but Lisa had to give it up in 2004 because of her work schedule.

Lisa says it wasn't all that easy to make friends when they first came to Williams Lake, and they didn't have much social life until they joined fun ball. They played for the Red Dog League's Jockey Cadillacs, which morphed into the Red Dog Rippers, and Lisa was league president. The two also played for the Shrewz in the Williams Lake Slo-Pitch League. In January 2009 they went to Cuba with two teams, the Rowdies and the Lakers, and in March 2011 they were part of a fifteen-team contingent that went to Jamaica for a slo-pitch tournament. They came home with a bronze medal. Alyx and Patrick, both graduates of Williams Lake Secondary, played on the Red Dog Rippers team with them as well as for different teams in the slo-pitch league.

After three years in sales, then management, at Consumer's Carpet, Lisa enrolled at the local Thompson Rivers University campus for the computer certificate course. It was a heavy load, and she did eleven courses in five and a half months. "Making the course deadlines certainly prepared me for the stress of meeting newspaper deadlines," she says.

She worked for the William Lake Hearing Clinic before joining the *Tribune* staff. She found newspaper work challenging but she had a great list of customers and says that made it all worthwhile.

As publisher, Lisa oversees a staff of sixteen in editorial, advertising, production and the front office. She represents the paper at numerous functions, and occasionally takes part in some front-line jobs, such as taking a paper delivery route on Carrier Appreciation Day.

Alyx lives in Williams Lake and is the mother of the Bowering's first grandchild, Ryden James. Patrick is in Edmonton where he has an apprenticeship with Finning as a certified heavy-duty Red Seal parts person.

Erin Hitchcock

Tribune editor Erin Hitchcock is Cariboo born and bred. She was born at Cariboo Memorial Hospital in 1981 and lived in the Dog Creek Road area until she was four, when she moved to the Miocene area with her mother and sister and they started a farm.

"My sister and I grew up on ten acres around chickens, horses, dogs, cats and goats, and the occasional sheep and turkey," she says. She became interested in journalism as a teenager. " I enjoyed reading, writing and English over math and sciences, and I was, and still am, interested in learning about a wide variety of things happening in the world around me."

After taking a few arts courses at the University College of the Cariboo (now TRU), she went to work for the *Cariboo Advisor* as a reporter. She was there for a few months in the summer of 2003 before moving to Vancouver. In 2004, she enrolled in Langara College's journalism diploma program, and began a journalism internship at the *Burnaby NOW/The Record* newspaper as a reporter. After completing her internship and graduating from the journalism program, Erin stayed at the paper on a temporary basis. She knew the position would be cut, and in January 2008 she began to think about going home to Williams Lake.

"Vancouver was a great experience, but I have always been a country-and-nature-loving girl. I was tired of the traffic and I missed Williams Lake and its beautiful surrounding areas. The city parks in the Lower Mainland just didn't quite do it for me," she says.

She also wanted to be closer to her family, but she wasn't sure what she was going to do when she did get home. As luck would have it , she heard about a reporter's job at the *Tribune* and applied for it. She was still working at the *NOW/The Record* when *Tribune* editor Ken MacInnis interviewed her over the phone and soon after offered her the job. She came home in February to start her job with the paper. In November 2010, Ken left the *Tribune* to work for the city, and Erin took over the editor's desk.

When not on the job, she likes to garden, camp, hike and travel, not necessarily in that order. When she is not doing any of those things she is working on building a house with her boyfriend.

Gaylene Desautels and Anne Blake

*I*n terms of time served, production manager Gaylene Desautels is the senior staff person at the *Tribune*. She began working part-time as a typesetter after school, and joined the staff full-time in 1974 after stepping in to replace a staffer who was on medical leave. She moved from typesetting to composing, and took her five-year journeyman training under then shop foreman Dan Waldie.

Gaylene and Anne Blake almost come as a set, as they have been working together since Anne joined the production team in 1978. Anne did her five-year apprenticeship under Gaylene. She'd planned to go back to school, but the journeyman's wages convinced her to stay with the newspaper.

Gaylene is a true Williams Laker. She is a descendant of William Pinchbeck, who came to the Cariboo in 1860 as a police constable and stayed to establish a farm on the land that is now the city. His gravesite is on the hillside overlooking the stampede grounds. In Grade 1 Gaylene had the Marie Sharpe Gym as her classroom, and she later attended Crescent Heights, Kwaleen, Williams Lake Junior Secondary and Columneetza Senior Secondary.

Anne came from North Vancouver with her family when Gibraltar mines opened in the early 1970s, and her dad's company Wismer and Rawlings opened an office there. Anne was in Grade 11 and she was upset over the move. "I cried all the way up here," she says, "I didn't want to leave Vancouver for a cowtown."

She soon settled in. After graduating from Columneetza she spent a year at the *Tribune* as a typesetter, then went to Simon Fraser University for a year. She came home, got married, and when her son was two years old she went back to the *Tribune* part-time. On her first day back on the job she worked a twelve-hour shift, and she did wonder about the part-time bit. There weren't many long shifts but they did happen when there were bigger than usual newspapers or extra supplements. A thirty-plus-page broadsheet edition would challenge the production staff to meet the press deadlines.

Neither Gaylene nor Anne had to worry about daycare. When Gaylene's son Jordan arrived he was cared for by his grandparents while she was working, and Anne's sister Jill had a son the same age as Dusty, and he stayed with her.

The jobs in the production room were very different when Gaylene and Anne began. The days of typesetting and cutting and pasting are long gone. In the good old days, the editorial staff used typewriters to type their stories onto paper and the typesetters retyped it. The Compugraphic equipment used in the 1970s was unforgiving. It was a complicated procedure using a spinning filmstrip and lights that flashed the images onto light-sensitive paper and then it had to be developed. Once it was done it was done, and there was no way to correct mistakes. Later the copy was typed onto disks, but it still had to be developed.

One big change that came in the late 1980s was the "Advantage," touted as state-of-the-art equipment. It was the first attempt to go desktop but it was so cumbersome the production crew called it the "Disadvantage." They did ad layouts at the huge Advantage station, and there were so many complicated commands it took forever to create an ad. Pregnant operators were required to wear lead vests they got from the dental clinic. One day they did a test with Gaylene on the Advantage and Anne on the Compugraphic machine and found the old system was faster.

The *Tribune* went to a complete desktop system in 2002. No more grid sheets, exacto knives, wax, line gauges and reduction wheels, although Gaylene and Anne have kept the tools for old-time's sake.

One of the biggest changes has been in makeup of ads. Advertisers used to have a limited choice of graphics that came from a few layout books. Now with the huge variety provided by graphic companies via the Internet, there is virtually no limit to ad design. Even with the technology and the *Tribune* now being a tabloid newspaper instead of broadsheet, there are still five part-time to full-time people on the ad-design team.

The *Tribune* has the capacity to print a number of local papers. It prints the *Ashcroft Journal*, and Anne does the ad design and layout for that paper now.

Along with sharing an office, Gaylene and Anne both enjoy the outdoors. Gaylene has been skiing since 1974. She also does scrapbooking and enjoys gardening. She and husband Mark have a travel trailer they make good use of in the summer months. They enjoy skiing and vacationing with their two children, Taylor, who is the chief cook at the Bean Counter, and Jordan, who is employed at Stampede Glass.

Anne works three days a week unless she is covering vacation time for someone. She also likes to ski. She and her husband, Flip, enjoy the outdoors and like to hike and travel, and they also enjoy spending time at their cabin on Quesnel Lake. Anne has two grandchildren and four step-grandchildren. Her son Dusty Rhodes is a journeyman pressman with Black Press, and he's on his way to becoming a company veteran. He started in the mailroom in 1992 after school, and before that he had a paper route.

Mary Langstrom

Mary Langstrom started her twenty-eight-year career with the *Tribune* working in the front office. Within six months she was offered a job on the production crew, and she did a four-year apprenticeship under Gaylene. "The *Tribune* had a young staff at the time, and we spent time together on and off work," Mary says.

In 2000 the newspaper began to do more with computers, and there was less work for staff. Mary was never laid off, but her hours "were getting pretty sketchy" when she was offered a job as a graphic artist building ads. There was no apprenticeship or formal training for this, and she would have to learn on the job. Mary, who works part-time, says the job has changed dramatically since she began. She says there is so much material available on the Internet, the sky's the limit for ads.

She came to Williams Lake in 1972 when the District Forest Office opened and her dad transferred from Port Alberni as inspector of log scaling. She went to school here for six years, then returned to Port Alberni when her dad transferred back. Her sister stayed in Williams Lake, and when Mary finished school, she came back and stayed, got married and started a career with the *Tribune*. She and husband Arne live at Rose Lake where they have summer activities at their doorstep and enjoy spending time with their extended family.

Gaeil Farrar

by Gaeil Farrar

Tribune journalist Gaeil Farrar has been writing stories about other people since 1980, so it is appropriate for her to tell her own story.

One of the more thrilling times of my life was spending a winter washing dishes in a luxury hotel in Zermatt, Switzerland. On one particularly beautiful day off, a group of us decided to ski into Cervinia, Italy, for lunch. About seven tows, chairs, and a gondola or two took us to the top of the mountain under the famed Matterhorn where we would start our ski. Those who had made the trip before warned us to be extra careful skiing the narrow gullies roped off with yellow flags on one side.

We had a magnificent spaghetti lunch. Riding the lifts back up I realized how close I was to real danger. On the other side of those tiny flags were sheer cliffs dropping off hundreds or perhaps thousands of feet to certain death.

Back in my room I fell asleep, exhausted but deliriously content. An hour later I awoke with pain in my eyes. My eyelids felt like sandpaper ripping across my eyeballs. Stupidly I had forgotten my sunglasses and was experiencing severe snow blindness. For the next couple of hours I lay in my darkened room with my eyes wide open, unblinking, to prevent more pain. Finally my roommates came home with some aspirin so I could get some sleep and heal.

That experience kind of sums up my life—great, wonderful experiences with many challenges, interspersed with intense pain, and not always of the physical variety. I started out as an optimist convinced I wanted to learn and experience everything there is to know about the world. But like most people, the more tragedy I saw and experienced the less I wanted to be "out there," as they say. Hence my slow evolution from mover and shaker to watcher and recorder.

There are many adventures I could tell about—like the time I came face to face with Prince Rainier waving and smiling at me with his elegant wife Grace beside him; being invited into the pits with Jackie Stewart at the Grand Prix in Monaco; swimming with giant turtles in Hawaii; finding an red frog thought to be extinct in

Costa Rica; falling out of a window and breaking my wrist; meeting Dizzy Gillespie at the Montreaux Jazz Festival; picking peaches topless (it was very hot); learning to play bridge; making my first coat; the thrill of singing and acting in a musical... so much to do, so little time.

I grew up in a middle-class family with three younger brothers and parents who refused to take on any debt. Except for one trip with the Brownies to Port Angeles, I spent my entire childhood in Victoria and on Vancouver Island. We hiked and camped all over the island but could never afford to go to the mainland, so when graduation time came I was more than eager to see the world.

I had two talents: writing and art. Fortunately I have found my way into both worlds with a lot of hard work in the business world. After taking on various jobs in Cranbrook and Kimberley I landed an excellent job with CP Rail in Trail. After a year there I bid on a night job in Nelson where I spent seven years working afternoon and night shifts while attending art school and university during the day. No ketchup soup for me.

At one point I was a three-car family all on my own—motorcycle, van and VW beetle—which were all very old, mind you, and was also able to fit in some travelling.

Marrying a teacher brought me to Williams Lake where I enjoyed getting to know this vibrant arts community and make pottery at home for a few years.

The Cariboo is an odd place for me to end up given my inherent fear of guns, riding horses, grizzly bears and cougars. Needless to say you won't find me tromping through the bush without a well-armed guide. But during my years here I have had some amazing encounters with wildlife and the humans who live and thrive here.

Ironically there are twists and turns in the story about how I ended up at the *Tribune*. My roommate, a fledging reporter with the *Trail Daily Times,* who would later spend time reporting for the *Tribune*, wrote about me as the first female CP Rail car checker since the Second World War. Just as ironically, a friend from art school in Nelson was working as the *Tribune* photographer when I went looking for a job, ostensibly to earn enough money to buy my own kiln. I had been using the guild kiln. She encouraged me to apply for a job as the *Tribune*'s community editor. Coming to the *Tribune* I became hooked on writing, and left pottery behind to learn another craft which would also mean working long hours and weekends. And so here I am thirty years later, divorced, no kids and living vicariously through the stories of others.

A woman from Russia I once met at a conference in Caux, Switzerland, asked me what I collected. I thought the question rather odd and just stared at her unable to answer. Then she said: "I know, you collect people."

It's true, I guess—I love people and their stories.